THE ROYAL FJORD

Also by Ray Phillips

The Little Green Valley

Two Native loggers with a nice catch. COURTESY BEA SWANSON

THE ROYAL FJORD

Memories of Jervis Inlet

Ray Phillips

HARBOUR PUBLISHING

1 2 3 4 5 — 19 18 17 16 15

Harbour Publishing Co. Ltd.
P.O. Box 219, Madeira Park, BC, V0N 2H0
www.harbourpublishing.com

Edited by Betty Keller
Indexed by Brianna Cerkiewicz
Front cover photo by Dean van't Schip. Back cover top photo by the author. Back cover bottom photo courtesy Linda Mattis.
Cover design by Brianna Cerkiewicz
Text design by Mary White
Printed and bound in Canada

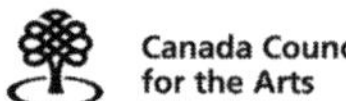

Harbour Publishing acknowledges the support of the Canada Council for the Arts, which last year invested $157 million to bring the arts to Canadians throughout the country. We also gratefully acknowledge financial support from the Government of Canada through the Canada Book Fund and from the Province of British Columbia through the BC Arts Council and the Book Publishing Tax Credit.

Cataloguing data available from Library and Archives Canada
ISBN 978-1-55017-708-4 (paper)
ISBN 978-1-55017-709-1 (ebook)

For Jack Gooldrup

Contents

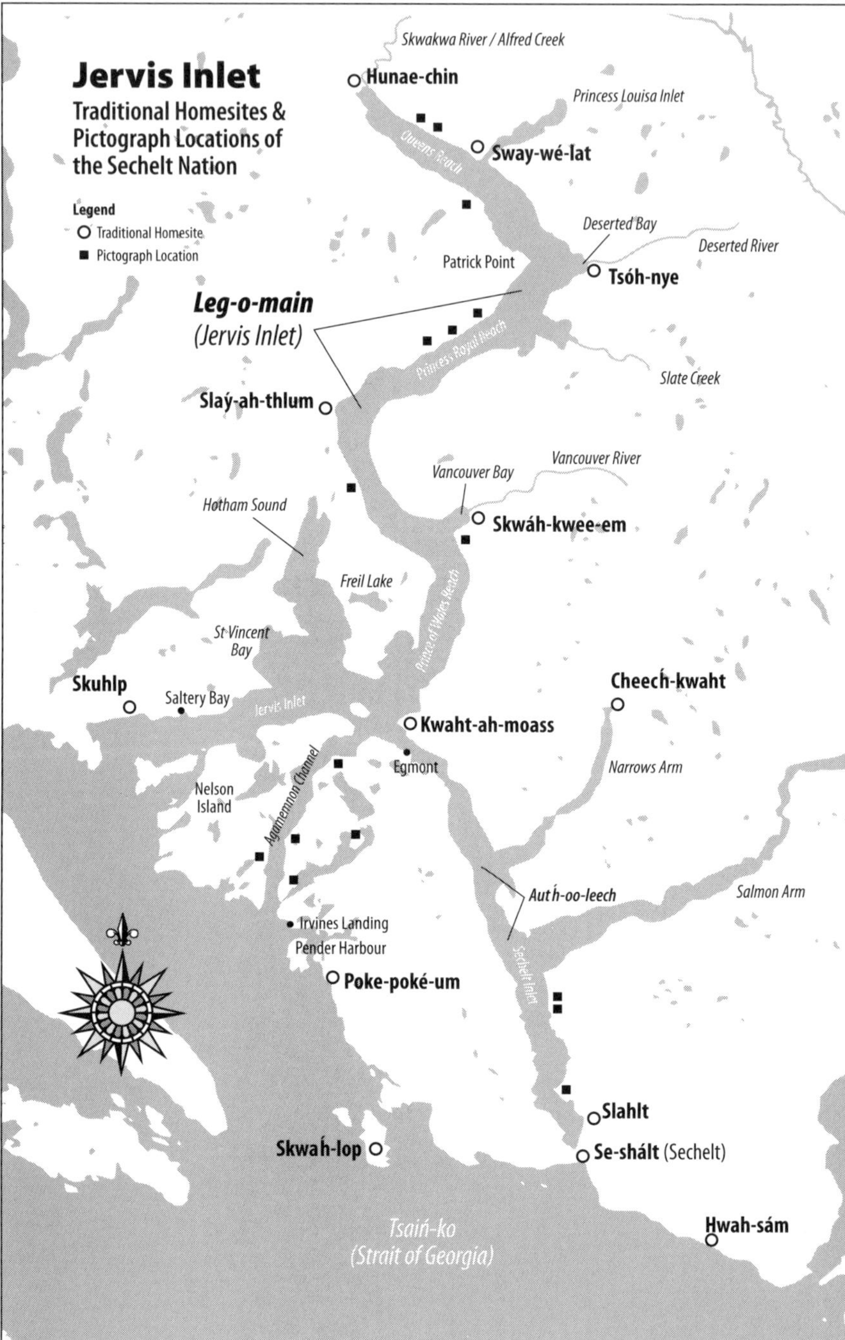

Jervis Inlet
Traditional Homesites & Pictograph Locations of the Sechelt Nation
Legend
Traditional Homesite
Pictograph Location
Skwakwa River / Alfred Creek
Hunae-chin
Princess Louisa Inlet
Queens Reach
Sway-wé-lat
Deserted Bay
Deserted River
Patrick Point
Tsóh-nye
Leg-o-main
(Jervis Inlet)
Princess Royal Reach
Slate Creek
Slaý-ah-thlum
Vancouver River
Vancouver Bay
Hotham Sound
Skwáh-kwee-em
Freil Lake
Prince of Wales Reach
St Vincent Bay
Cheecȟ-kwaht
Skuhlp
Saltery Bay
Jervis Inlet
Kwaht-ah-moass
Egmont
Narrows Arm
Nelson Island
Agamemnon Channel
Auťh-oo-leech
Salmon Arm
Irvines Landing
Pender Harbour
Sechelt Inlet
Poke-poké-um
Slahlt
Skwaȟ-lop
Se-shált (Sechelt)
Tsaiń-ko
(Strait of Georgia)
Hwah-sám

Introduction

Around 1919 my dad, James William Phillips, moved from Victoria to Jervis Inlet to work in a logging camp, and over his long life of living and working there he gathered stories. He passed these stories on to me, and because he often told the same ones over again, that is most likely why I remember them. The facts never changed with the telling, so I guess they are mostly true. Many are just humorous anecdotes but others tell some of the history of this inlet, and if someone doesn't record them, they will be lost to future generations. I think that would be a shame.

Dad started writing down his life's story in longhand, but he didn't get it finished before he passed away at seventy-seven years from lung cancer. He smoked all his life. I promised him that I would do my best to finish it, and I did. I had Dad's story all typed up and sent it around to many of the cousins. A lot of that material is in this book. Some other stories were gleaned from old-timers and residents of Pender Harbour and Egmont, some are just good stories of the general area of Jervis Inlet, and some are based on my own personal experiences from the years I spent working and exploring in this beautiful fjord. As most stories about Jervis Inlet involve the logging industry, I have been very fortunate to get some of the folks that were either witnesses or the descendants of the early pioneer families to write their memories and supply some photos—like Kevin Newcombe's stories of old Charlie Newcombe and his steam donkeys and Bea Swanson's picture of two logging trucks moving a 140-foot spar tree.

But this book is by no means a history of the Jervis area, because that would take a knowledge far beyond my limited resources to record. In talking to Billy Griffith about it, I am forced to realize just how little I know about the history of places like Egmont, so with my dad's help I just recorded what we know. And maybe the few who read this will be inspired to put down some of what I've missed.

Each section is written as a short story, so don't look for a pattern. Some stories are linked together in a limited way to help you better understand the circumstances. And the accuracy of the facts are only as good as what I got from the person who told me his or her story. I have discarded some stories that I thought were off. I apologize if I have offended anyone. It was not at all intentional. If you were missed, it might be because I didn't feel qualified to tell a story, and I purposely passed on it. After all, as I stated, this is only a collection of short stories and not a history. That will have to wait for someone else to tackle at some later date.

—Ray Phillips

Jervis Inlet

Jervis Inlet, the deepest of any inlet on the BC coast, is over forty nautical miles long, with many side bays and inlets such as Sechelt Inlet, Princess Louisa Inlet and Hotham Sound branching off it. The tidal water flows in and out on both sides of Hardy Island and through Agamemnon Channel, which lies between Nelson Island and the Sechelt Peninsula. Pender Harbour is a mile from the southeast end of Jervis Inlet so it's part of this story, too.

Jervis Inlet could be called the Royal Fjord because when the British came, they named many of its reaches, mountains and inlets for British royalty, barons and lords. Many of them were named by Captain George Vancouver when he surveyed Georgia Strait and Vancouver Island in his search for the Northwest Passage in 1792. Captain George Henry Richards of the Royal Navy, who was sent from England to survey the BC coast in HMS *Plumper*, named most of the surrounding peaks after Queen Victoria's many children. When he ran out of royals, he named bays and inlets after the ships in Admiral Horatio Nelson's fleet. Captain Daniel Pender finished Richards' survey of the Sunshine Coast and Jervis Inlet in the summer of 1860.

Native Footprints

According to Lester Peterson in his book *The Story of the Sechelt Nation* (Harbour, 1990), Jervis Inlet in the language of the Sechelt people is Leg(K)0h'Main. There are many signs of Native activity here, but most people visiting Jervis will want to have a look at the pictographs on the rock bluff just below the BC Ferry terminal at Earls Cove in Agamemnon Channel. These fairly bright red rock paintings have been there for several hundred years, much longer than any of our modern paints can last. My friend Jimmy Johnson, son of Chief Dan of the Garden Bay reserve, says it was a secret formula, but some of the ingredients were oil of salmon eggs, blood and a red clay that came from the Skwakwa River area at the head of Jervis Inlet, possibly cinnabar, a form of mercury sulfide.

But the Earls Cove pictograph gallery is only one of many in Jervis. My friend Jack Gooldrup of Gibsons made many trips up the inlet trying to find the location of all the pictograph galleries, and when he was finished he could take you to twenty sites. Many of these were unknown to Basil Joe, who was chosen by the Sechelt elders as the storyteller or keeper of their nation's oral history. Basil was raised at

Deserted Bay (Tsonei or Ts'unay) and could remember the annual migration of Native people from Squamish over the trail through the Elaho River valley. (Reggie Paul was chosen to succeed Basil, and he sometimes accompanied them on Jack Gooldrup's trips up Jervis.)

The site Jack showed me in 1962 is in Queens Reach about two or three miles beyond the entrance to Princess Louisa Inlet. There are two galleries there not too far apart, but unless the tide is very high, you may require some kind of a ladder as the beach is very steep. This was the place where the Native people brought their "soul stones." Before the white man came and introduced the people to a new religion, the medicine man or shaman would paint a sign on a small, flat, palm-sized, egg-shaped rock that was chosen by a young person as part of the puberty rites of entry into adulthood. They were to keep that rock all their lives because their souls were supposed to be inside their rock. After someone died, the people built a big fire on top of their stone and when the stone was red hot, they threw water on it, which cracked it open to let the soul go free. I think Jack may have got this information directly from Basil because in his book, Peterson just calls them soul stones but gives no further explanation. But Peterson wasn't there for all the many trips that Jack and Basil took up the inlet.

When we went there in 1962, there was a great pile of the stones still there, not one of them whole, and you could still see the paint on a few of them even after they had gone through the fire. Jack said this was a special place and this big pile of stones was fired in a secret shaman ceremony to let the souls of living people go free before the Catholic priests could confiscate the stones; the priests forbade them to practise this ceremony, along with the potlatch, because they called it witchcraft. And the Native people were ready to try anything the priests said because of the fear they associated with all the epidemics, where up to 90 percent of the people in some villages died over just a few years. On top of this, the white man's government imposed severe penalties for continuing the potlatch. The priests forbade this stone practice. The government didn't understand the significance of stripping the Natives of their culture, language and identity as a people and how this would lead to the social problems we see today. Hopefully the present revival of Native culture will help to give them back their dignity and their recognition as a distinct people.

Jack Gooldrup took a real interest in this project and spent countless days at much personal expense locating all the other galleries and sacred sites in Jervis. With the exception of Les Peterson's mention of Jack's help in his book, he never received much recognition for all the many trips he made in his boat to take old Basil Joe and a guy named Fletcher and often Les Peterson himself to find the pictograph galleries. Old Basil died soon after he made these trips, so we had come close to losing all this history and the Native place names.

Another close call for some of the precious history of this area came after an English couple, Amy and Francis Barrow, died in Victoria. They had cruised the Coast during the Depression years, making the most complete record of Native pictographs and petroglyphs in existence, but after they died, the people who were cleaning out their house dumped cartons of their papers onto a big bonfire. Some of their logbooks and photos were caught in time, and they have been preserved in the Campbell River Museum for future generations. When I was there last year, only a few of Francis Barrows' photos were on display; the rest are on file. They are only black and white but of good quality for their age. Their whole story is recorded in the book *Upcoast Summers* by Beth Hill (Horsdal & Schubart, 1985).

One year my dad was a part of a crew that was hired to take out cedar logs and telephone poles at the left side of the head of Hotham Sound. I think the name of the company was Baxter Pole Company. But when they tried to fall some of the trees, it wasn't long before the fallers had their saws dulled in the cut. They thought it was rocks, but when they chopped in, they found human bones. It seems the Natives would pull back the bark to remove enough wood to get a body in and then fasten the bark back, and the tree eventually grew over the scar. The company had to pull out because no one would work in a Native burial ground.

My Dad's Story

When my dad started writing his life's story, he began with his memories of his life in Kent, England, where he was born in November 1905. His father immigrated to Canada first, and in the middle of winter 1911 my grandma and their five kids—my dad and his four sisters—sailed for Canada on the old *Empress of Ireland.* It was a rough trip that finished on one engine, and most of the passengers, including my grandmother and aunts, were seasick all the way across. Dad said he never missed a meal in the dining room, which was nearly empty. He mentioned that Princess Louise, daughter of Queen Victoria, was on the ship and helped to nurse a sailor who had fallen from the rigging. I have since read that she did this kind of thing, which didn't please her mother, who thought her daughter should be above helping the wounded. (That ship sank about three years later in the St. Lawrence after colliding with a Norwegian ship; more than a thousand lives were lost.)

Grandma and the kids landed in Halifax and came by train to the Fraser Valley where Dad's father had a job at Ross's Mill on Mount Lehman Road. At that time it was just a straight cut through the huge cedars and fir trees, except where the scattered settlers had cleared a bit of land. Dad said the family was so ignorant about this new country that a few weeks after they got settled the girls came running in to tell their dad that there was a cow out in the yard with a tree on its head. Their dad knew what it was, but by the time he got a gun and shells together the big buck deer had disappeared. He used a huge stump, nearly ten feet across, as the base to build a woodshed on. Dad and his school-aged sisters (three more children were born after the family came to Canada) had to walk nearly three miles to the Pine Grove School. They later moved to Vancouver Island with a relative who had encouraged the family's move from England.

When Dad was about eleven years of age, Grandpa joined the new Canadian Navy, so Dad had to quit school after he finished grade four at Metchosin School outside Victoria. The school is now a museum, and I've seen his name in the registry there. He started working for a farmer who did some logging with a single drum yarding steam capstan. By the time he was twelve, Dad's job was to drive the big horse that pulled the mainline up to three hundred feet back into the woods and follow the log out then haul the choker back for another log. In December 1917 Grandpa was on the training ship HMCS *Niobe*, which was one of the ships that was badly shattered in the Halifax Harbour Explosion, and he was wounded and sent back home to heal in Victoria. After this he began doing road work, but he was not the same man as before, and his behaviour brought about the end of my grandparents' marriage.

In 1920 my grandma moved with her eight kids to Goliath Bay in Jervis Inlet where her future son-in-law, Charlie Sundquist, had built a large house. After a while an old bachelor named Tom Robinson proposed to her, and she

Tom Robinson and Dad's mother Clara Phillips never married but lived together for nearly twenty years.
COURTESY PHILLIPS FAMILY COLLECTION

and the kids all moved into his big house in St. Vincent Bay, southwest of Hotham Sound. Divorces were very expensive for people of slim means, so they decided to just live together, and it was an arrangement that lasted until my grandma died of cancer nearly twenty years later, after they had moved to Pender Harbour.

With the arrival of the six school-aged Phillips kids plus the kids that already lived there, a school was now viable, so a teacher, Miss Chasney, was sent to teach there in one of the old houses. My dad, who was now the breadwinner for the whole family and worked logging and fishing, had to register as a student just to keep the school open. Sometimes he had to go back to Vancouver Island to find work, and later he always told of the awful living conditions in some of those camps before the woodworkers union got some influence and forced the companies to bring in better living conditions and safety regulations. But he said even the threat of the unions coming in caused things to get a lot better. The loggers lived in big bunkhouses with triple-decker bunks all around the walls and a big drum heater in the centre where they all hung their wet clothes and socks on lines to dry for the next day. The smell was not too appealing.

He said you got to wash your clothes on Sundays in hot water that was boiled in big copper boilers out in the yard. It took a rolling boil to kill the body lice and bedbugs. Some guys didn't wash their clothes and everyone suffered. If a man was hurt, unless it was serious, he had to wait until quitting time before he got attention. If a man was killed, the body was not taken out until the crummy went in to camp at day's end.

When Dad first began logging in Jervis Inlet, about 1919, he and his future brother-in-law Charlie Sundquist worked for the Booth Logging Company that had a railroad outfit around Freil Lake on the peninsula of land between Hotham Sound and Prince of Wales Reach. This was before Grandma and the rest of the Phillips family came over from Victoria, so he and Charlie were batching. Charlie, who was Swedish, didn't mind the taste of old coffee and he liked the convenience of always having a cup ready without waiting for it to brew, so he kept the pot simmering on the back of the stove. They would add fresh coffee every few days and empty the grounds when the pot was getting too full. One day they found the complete skeleton of a mouse in it, and no one had even noticed the enhanced flavour.

Booth snubbed the cars of logs down a steep railroad track into Goliath Bay, but that company seemed to be plagued by disaster. Once they were snubbing two railroad cars of logs down the last steep pitch, which was over a thousand feet, when the fastening broke between the cars and this huge snubbing machine that was way up the hillside, and the cars got going so fast that Dad figured they went halfway across the inlet underwater. The logs came popping up like breaching whales, but he figured the rail cars are still where they landed to this day.

The summer of 1921 was very hot and dry with everyone in Booth's camp on early shift to minimize the fire risk, but one day a fire started in the dry slash on the mountainside and the flames spread quickly. Dad was put in charge of the pumps on a float in the lake that supplied water for a number of hoses. As the fire advanced, all the mice, rats and birds were swimming and flying past him out into the lake, but some of the birds were so confused that they turned around and flew back into the flames and perished. The crew saved what they could of the company's equipment, but many machines and a lot of felled and bucked timber with many cold deck piles of logs were burnt up. This was too much for the company, and it put them out of business at that location, so Dad was looking for a job.

Sometimes Dad worked with his stepfather, Tom Robinson, at handlogging and horse logging on Tom's own property and on nearby government claims, though in those early days in Jervis Inlet most of the industry was handlogging because the steep shores made it easy to slide the trees into the saltchuck. For a few dollars the Forest Service would grant you the rights to handlog a mile of shoreline. You needed a big logging jack, usually a Gilchrist or Ellingsen, which were about two feet long with a two-foot-plus handle that weighed a little more than sixty pounds. These jacks had a big hooked foot for lifting a log that had nosed into the ground and stuck there, and at the top of the jack was a sharp, swivelled jaw that would bite into the end of a log to lift or push it. So with a crosscut saw, an axe, a spring board or two, a few boom chains and log dogs, a rowboat and a partner, you could go logging.

Dad told me a couple of stories that went the rounds about handloggers. The first one was about two men who got together an outfit and a claim in the inlet, and they moved around in a big sixteen-foot, double-ended rowboat. Maybe it was the isolation and the lack of other company, but after years of working in harmony they began to get on each other's nerves and quarrel over the slightest thing. This went on until they began to hate each other and couldn't stand to work together at all. So they agreed to divide everything right down the middle, even the double-ended rowboat, which they sawed in half to make two eight-foot boats. They nailed a stern onto each half and went their separate ways.

The other story was about a man who for some reason (perhaps like the former guys) found himself handlogging all alone. Common sense would tell you that apart from being a lot harder and less efficient, this was also very dangerous. Any work in the woods has a higher accident rate than almost any other occupation plus less chance of getting help when you don't see a soul for days at a time. Knowing this should have been enough deterrent to anyone, but this man—most likely against his better judgment—found himself working alone on his handlogging claim way up in the wilds of Jervis Inlet. It seems he had run some trees down the slope, and they had nosed into the beach below half tide, and he had to jack them up to put skids under them to slide them into the water. Somehow when he had one of these trees jacked up, the jack slipped out and the tree came down, pinning his foot under the tree, and the jack landed too far away for him to reach it. The tide was out, but unless he could get free, he was doomed to drown in a few hours when the tide came in. So he was forced to cut off his own foot.

All he had to work with was his axe and a pocket knife, but he would have had experience with butchering deer and known where he could cut without sawing through bone. Most likely he would have made a tourniquet with his shirt or something, using the axe handle or a stick to twist it, and after probably passing out a few times from the pain, he somehow managed to cut off his foot with his jackknife. Then he crawled into his rowboat where he still had to row many miles for help. He was extremely lucky to have survived his ordeal and lived to tell the tale.

There is another story out of Jervis that is very similar but doesn't involve the threat of drowning. This one happened years later than Dad's version because by this time the hospital was built in Pender Harbour, which didn't happen till August 1930. So maybe there were two incidents of that kind.

When Dad wasn't logging, he would go to Lasqueti Island for June and July to fish for blueback (young coho salmon) just like Bertrand Sinclair wrote in his novel *Poor Man's Rock* (Little, Brown, 1920). Dad had a small fishboat with a two-cycle gas engine that had a unique way to get it to reverse. Coming in for a landing, you held the "off" button down until the motor was on its last revolution, turned the timer over then released the stop button to give it the spark, and it would run backwards and stop the boat. One winter he was partners with Frank Silvey of Egmont, who was the son of Portuguese Joe Silvey's son, Joe Silvey II of Egmont. He and Dad longlined for bottom fish—some cod but mostly the small sharks called dogfish—on Frank's boat, the *Francis Point*. They averaged a ton a day and got seven dollars a ton. Big money in those days. When he was in his early seventies, Frank passed away while fishing on the *Francis Point*, but his wife, Vi, was able to bring the boat home into Deep Bay where he had a house out on the Deep Bay Spit. About ten years ago

I saw the *Francis Point* in Chemainus; it was still fishing cod and was still in its original condition as if Frank Silvey had just stepped off it.

Hotham Sound

For most people the most outstanding thing about Hotham Sound is the big falls that tumble from Freil Lake in tiers about 1,450 feet, falling almost directly into the waters of the sound. Though there are many beautiful waterfalls along the coast of BC, I think this one is the most spectacular. It is really something to sit in your boat in front of it when there is a big runoff. You will not soon forget it. My dad told me that when he first came there it was a good place to fish for big spring salmon in November. He would go over there in a rowboat and troll in the moonlight with a silver spoon on a handline, and sometimes he would get half a dozen or more.

Farther up the sound, still on the falls side and halfway to Lena Lake, is a lovely beach that Dad called Baker's Beach. The only thing he remembered about old man Baker was that he was a miserable old guy, but he died or moved away quite early on. Next to a nice, low-level piece of foreshore property with grass on it there was a gently shelving beach, and the whole community would meet there in the summer for a picnic. But disaster struck one summer when a young couple lost their year-old baby. Everyone was out of the water, eating or playing

The falls in Hotham Sound tumble 1,450 feet. AUTHOR COLLECTION

games, but the baby was wading in shallow water a few feet out from shore. The mother was sitting on the beach close by watching. She turned away for a few seconds, and when she looked again, the child was gone. Soon everyone was looking. They looked all over the water in front of the beach, and in spite of the fact that the water was crystal clear, there was no sign of the child. My dad said that a huge ling cod, about five feet long, was seen in ten feet of water, and he thought it might have swallowed the kid. That's not too far-fetched when ling cod bigger than a hundred pounds were caught there in those days, and one this size would have a tooth-lined mouth the size of a deck bucket. There is a picture of a seventy-plus-pound ling cod in *Spilsbury's Album* (Harbour Publishing, 1990). I have caught a twenty-five-pounder that had swallowed my first fish, which was a ten-pounder. As far as Dad remembers, there were no more picnics on Baker's Beach.

Different logging ventures have worked this area over the years, some successfully and others not so well. Freil Lake had a lot of beautiful old-growth cedar, and a Japanese-Canadian company that supplied the Green Bay Shingle Mill put in a big crew of shingle bolt cutters. They filled the lake with bolts, and to get them to salt water, about a thousand feet lower, they built a flume that descended over top of the big falls. You can still see where it passed to the left of the falls on a steep gradient down to the camp not far from the Harmony Islands. That flume had many problems, so when it burned up (arson by racist elements was suspected), the owners couldn't afford to rebuild it.

My dad said that when the operation was going well, there was a guy named Sandy who threatened to ride a log down the flume. Dad felt the guy was playing with a few cards short of a full deck. Anyway, one day after the crew left, Sandy pushed a hollow-butted cedar log into the flume, climbed into the hollow and away he went for the ride of his life—or almost his death. It seems that, after free-falling the last few feet, the log stopped abruptly when it hit the water and rammed him way into the hollow. Luckily one of the cooks saw his head sticking out or he would have drowned. The cook alerted the crew and they were able to extricate him, but he had to be sent to a Vancouver hospital where it took months to get all the slivers out of him. (I heard another story that it was Steve Johnstone who went for a ride on a big cedar slab, encouraged to do so by his brothers, so maybe there were two slivery rides.) For years after the shingle bolt company quit there were lots of bolts still floating around the lake. There is now a good logging road into Freil Lake from Granville Bay.

I witnessed a strange phenomenon one night when Dad and I were anchored just off the big beach at the head of Hotham Sound. From all around the mountains, but mostly on the falls side, you could hear these loud sounds like when you release the air from a big compressor at the end of the day. About every five minutes there was a loud whoosh up in a mountain, which echoed around the bay. Dad had heard it several times before, and he called it air pockets. It was very scary, and it went on for about two hours. Billy Griffith thinks it could have been snow slides way up in the tops of the mountains.

Right out in front of Hotham Sound is the deepest place inside the continental shelf—perhaps in North America. It's four hundred fathoms deep there—almost half a mile—and for years there was a buoy anchored there because the calm waters of Jervis Inlet made it an ideal place to test the Pisces series of deep-sea submersibles. It is nearly as deep just off Lone Tree or Miller Island extending right up to Delta Rock's gravel operation in the main part of the inlet. Lone Tree Island got its local name from the nice straight fir tree, about two feet in diameter, that stood there. It was the widely held belief that one of the local handloggers needed a swifter for his boom and took it because the island is so small and smooth that the tree was a sure stumper into the chuck. Maybe another tree will take its place there in time and survive long enough to fulfill the name.

St. Vincent Bay

Most of the years that Dad's family lived in St. Vincent Bay their near neighbours were old Pete Day, Mr. and Mrs. Parsons and an old couple called Hiltze. There was also an old bachelor named Bob Herd who lived alongside Pete Day. His rules of hygiene were somewhat different. He never washed his dishes in the usual way. When he was finished eating, he would set the plate on the floor and Spot, his little dog, would lick it clean. Then old Bob would put the plate on the table upside down for the next meal. He made his money by selling dogfish oil to horse loggers for skid grease. He rendered the oil by boiling the livers in big cauldrons and skimming the oil off as it came up. The process worked better if the livers were aged for a few days, so the odours coming off his oil works were pretty bad. People going by kept complaining about the smell, and one day old Bob had enough. Dad said he was ladling the oil into four-gallon cans and he stopped, tipped up the ladle and took a healthy swig. "Dawgfish, Dawgfish! There's Dawgfish!" His complainers all disappeared to lose their last meal.

Old Bob's son worked as a purchasing agent for Woodward's Stores, and old Bob had quite a few prune trees.

Prunes—or, as every logger called them, "CPR strawberries"—were a favourite dessert in those days, so the market for them was always good. When the fruit was ripe and the weather was sunny, old Bob would pick all his prunes and lay them out in the sun to shrivel up and dry. This took several days and involved covering them up at night to keep the dew off. He had such a big area to cover that he had to use everything he could find, including his sheets and blankets, which were never washed for years. Dad always wondered what the customers' reaction would have been if they could see how their prunes were produced.

There was another old character who roamed all over the area getting by with no visible means of support. He had an old boat that was easily recognized, and every time he came for a visit, something of value went missing. He was very clever, and you considered yourself lucky if he didn't get you for something. In those days most loggers had a small freight shed on their floats where things could be left in the dry. It would have been an insult to your neighbours to put a lock on anything. Stuff could lie around for long periods and you would never lose a thing. But this old thief changed all that, and people would see him coming and hurry down to their floats to chase him away before he could tie up.

One guy was a little slow getting down to his float, and the old character's boat was already fastened to his float. A lot of boats that worked around logs had a weight on a line tied on at the middle of the boat, which they could hang over a log to hold the boat for a few minutes so the boat didn't drift away while they worked. So the logger gave the old thief a piece of his mind and told him to get out of there. The old guy pretended that his pride was wounded and said, "If that's the way you want it, I'm never coming back," and he pulled in his weight, put it on the deck of his boat and left in a big huff. As the boat went out of sight, and the logger was congratulating himself about getting rid of him without losing anything, he realized one of his boom chains was missing. The old guy had tied his line onto it and had been using it to hold his boat. It was worth quite a few bucks in those days.

The Hollingsworths

Across Hotham Sound at Granville Bay lived the Hollingsworths in their big family home. Henry Hollingsworth is first mentioned as a single logger living in the Discovery Passage area before the turn of the century, and he worked his way up to become very successful. About 1898 he took out his pre-emption at Granville Bay and built a lovely house that was big for those times. Mrs. Hollingsworth—her name was Levina—had one of the only pianos in the area, and she loved to entertain and see people have fun. Her guests always got the VIP treatment at mealtimes—white linen tablecloths and sterling silver. That house had a huge living room, so several times a year they held a dance there and people came from all over, and sometimes the party lasted till the wee hours and beyond. That big house was still in the bay when I was a boy.

Granville Bay was named after the Hollingsworths' oldest son, and the next bay out toward Captain Island is locally called Harry Bay after the other son, although it was also called Kinman's Bay for the old logger who lived there. (The Lapan Logging Company had started logging in this bay but after six months sold out to Booth Logging, who moved the operation over to Goliath Bay.) These two boys were raised in the house in Granville Bay. When they were pretty young, they went up the mountain behind the house and found a hole that had been drilled by a prospector years before. Nothing would do but they had to see if they could fire a projectile from this height, so they put a few sticks of powder in the hole, rammed

The Hollingsworth family. From left to right: Henry, Harry, Granville and Levina Elizabeth. COURTESY JANET (HOLLINGSWORTH) EAGLE

Mrs. Hollingsworth with her granddaughters and family friends. COURTESY JANET (HOLLINGSWORTH) EAGLE

The big house in Granville Bay. This photo was taken before Henry was killed. Note the chute and log booms. COURTESY JANET (HOLLINGSWORTH) EAGLE

them down, fitted the hole with a big wooden plug and drove it in. After lighting the fuse, they got clear, and many seconds after the explosion they saw the splash away out in the bay.

Henry Hollingsworth had a crew of men working for him at the time of his accidental death. The story goes that when the regular donkey puncher couldn't pull hard enough to dislodge a hung-up log, Hollingsworth got on the machine. By whipping the mainline so that it bowed up above a straight line and by using the speed of the steam engine and going ahead on the line as it came down, he got a lot more pull out of it, but it broke the line. The mainline wrapped all around him, killing him instantly. This was about 1916, when the boys were still young and at home.

Mrs. Hollingsworth lived on there for many more years. My Aunt Winnie worked for her when she was sick one time. Mrs. Hollingsworth was losing her hearing, and Aunt Winnie had to raise her voice to be heard. After that Aunt Winnie always raised her voice above normal, and continued to speak like this for the rest of her life. After Harry Hollingsworth married my dad's sister Annie, they moved to Stillwater, below Westview, and eventually they tore down the big house in Granville Bay and used the material to build Mrs. Hollingsworth a new house in the Stillwater area, or so I was

Harry and Annie Hollingsworth on their wedding day. COURTESY JANET (HOLLINGSWORTH) EAGLE

told. The original house was without a doubt the largest, finest one in the whole area, as you can see in the photos.

As my dad's five sisters grew into young women, it wasn't too long before there were lots of interested young bachelors coming around courting. His sisters Rosina, or Queenie as she was called by the family, and Winnie were the first to the altar. Queenie married Jimmie Johnson, a former sailor who was now a logging donkey engineer. They lived at St. Vincent Bay for a few years. Winnie married Charlie Sundquist, another donkey puncher, and they lived in Goliath Bay for the first years. The next to go was Florrie, who married John Herstead, a Norwegian logger, but it wasn't long before they moved to Vancouver. Then Harry Hollingsworth married Annie, and his brother Granville wed Pat, the last of the Phillips sisters.

For a while they all lived around St. Vincent Bay, and Dad told some funny stories of things that happened when

Left to right: Florrie, Queenie and Winnie on the beach at St. Vincent Bay.
COURTESY JANET (HOLLINGSWORTH) EAGLE

the whole family was still there. Granville had a good-sized boat, and one night he came and got my dad to go hunting for some fresh meat (there were no refrigerators in those days). They were going over to Nelson Island to pit-lamp a deer, which was strictly illegal. As Granville shone his

My dad's sister Winnie married Charlie Sundquist, a logging donkey engineer.
COURTESY ALMA SANFORD

Florrie married John Herstead, a Norwegian logger. From left to right: bridesmaid Claudia Gilpin, Aunt Florrie, John Herstead and my dad, Jim Phillips, as best man. COURTESY JANET (HOLLINGSWORTH) EAGLE

light ashore, a deer stuck its head up from behind a big windfall, so he took a shot and the head went down. But it popped up again, so he thought he must have missed and he fired again. The head went out of sight but came up in the same place. Now he thought his gun must be haywire, so he got another gun and fired again. This time the head stayed down. When he went ashore to get the deer, there were three dead deer.

There was a rock in St. Vincent Bay in front of the Robinsons' big house that dried at about six feet of tide. Dad was on the bow of Granville's boat ready to throw the anchor and thought they were getting close to the rock, so he voiced his concern to Granville, who was at the controls. Granville hollered back that he knew where every rock in the bay was. Just then they piled up on it. Quick as a wink Granville said,

"There's one now!" Luckily they were going very slow and were able to back off undamaged.

Another time Dad and Granville were coming in to anchor, and all Dad's sisters were watching from the verandah. My Aunt Florrie had given them a couple of loaves of fresh bread, and she had been saying how it had turned out extra good and light, and she was rightly proud of it. To have a little fun, Dad made a great show of tying the anchor line around the loaf of bread and throwing it over the bow, intimating how heavy it was. Florrie never let on that she saw this, and about a week later he found a dishrag cooked into his pancake.

Originally Granville and Harry Hollingsworth followed their dad into the logging business around Jervis Inlet, but eventually Harry moved to Stillwater, where he acquired his own outfit. He and Aunt Annie had five children and the three sons became loggers. The descendants of all five children have mostly settled in the Powell River area. Granville and Aunt Pat stayed around, and for a few years when their two kids were young they lived in Pender Harbour. Granville bought a big fish packer and freight boat called the *Patsco*, and they lived and worked on it for some years. Eventually he went on the tugs, mostly assisting booms through the Yuculta (also Euclataw) Rapids, and he worked at that till retirement. They moved to Quadra Island with their son, Lee, and daughter, Juanita, bought a farm and lived there the rest of their lives.

The Laughlin and Heid Families

The Laughlins and Heids logged together on Nelson Island, which sits like a huge plug in the entrance to Jervis Inlet. Their camp was at Cockle or Cockrill Bay, the only bay that affords shelter for booming logs between the point of Vanguard Bay and Captain Island off the east end of Nelson Island, and in the first years they used big horse teams and a chute to send their logs into the chuck. There were four Laughlin children—one boy, Earl Junior, and three girls, Pearl, Ruth and Clara or "Sis." The Heids were Charlie (who was born before his mother married Mr. Heid), Louie and Mary. After Mr. Heid drowned, his widow married a guy named Ibbotson. Louie Heid married Pearl Laughlin, and after Charlie Heid got out of the army, he married Ruth Laughlin. A while later Earl Laughlin Jr. married Mary Heid.

Louie and Pearl bought a steam donkey, put it on a big A-frame float and moved it into the Vanguard Bay area on Nelson Island. Pearl ran the donkey engine, and they were able to reach a thousand feet up the hillside and pull the logs directly into the saltchuck. Charlie also tried logging on his own with the same type of outfit. Old Earl Laughlin Sr. and

Top row, left to right: Reva Heid, Earl Laughlin Jr., Louis Heid, Ronald Heid, Henry Harris, Raleigh Heid, Charles Heid, Ruth (Laughlin) Heid, Clara (Laughlin) Harris ("Sis"). Middle row, left to right: Mary (Heid) Laughlin, Pearl (Laughlin) Heid, Clara Laughlin Sr., unknown. Bottom row, left to right: Delmer Laughlin, Velma Harris, Neil Laughlin, Marjory Harris.

COURTESY VELMA WALKER

his wife, Clara, split up and moved away, leaving Sis with her sister Pearl on the float camp. My dad got a job with Louie Heid, and he and Earl Laughlin Jr. became close friends.

Vanguard Bay

Walter Wray, his brother John and his two sisters came from England to Canada in 1910, and John Wray took a homestead on Nelson Island at Fearney Point, which is at the southeast end of the entrance to Agamemnon Channel. For a time Walter and his sister Amelia lived and worked in Egmont, and Walter became the magistrate for the whole Jervis area, recording births and deaths and such. Then he took on a good-sized piece of property at the end of Vanguard Bay on Nelson Island where he raised produce and poultry, which he sold at the Powell River mill site. Walter died about 1950, and when I lived in Vanguard for a few months in 1961 an old man named Oscar Orpana owned his place. In the early years a Mr. and Mrs. George Smith had a place behind the island that lies at the end of the bay and a family called Amscold lived nearby. The Smiths' place was where the community dances were sometimes held.

In 1961 my partner and I took on a timber claim that went from Rice Lake on the east side of Vanguard Bay up to the power line where it breaks over toward Agamemnon Channel, and we dumped and boomed behind the little island in the bay. That summer, to cut down on the daily travelling time from Pender Harbour, I rented a house from Art Marshall, who was working with Lew Milligan on the mountainside on the Blind Bay side of the island. I knew Art from 1946 when my dad and Uncle Pete Klein brought him to Cockburn Bay from Bond Sound, north of the entrance of Knight Inlet. They had rented all Art's logging equipment and had him do their booming for them. Then a few years after he worked for my dad and Uncle Pete, Art got a claim in Cockburn and operated on his own, but Charlie Klein was working in the same area, and the two of them got carried away in a bidding competition for timber. Marshall was the first to blink, and he sold out, put his new house on skids, moved it onto Milligan's Beach in Vanguard Bay and went to work with Lew Milligan. Art and his wife, Frances, and their two kids, Patty and Robert, moved into one of Milligan's camp houses where they were a lot more comfortable. Lew and Art would leave early in the morning in the camp boat, the *Vanguard*, for his Cat show around in Blind Bay. Somehow those two guys kept Lew's old International Harvester "corn binder" going until they had roads more than halfway to the top of the mountain. International Harvester had been just a farm machinery company at first, before they began making TD18 "cats," which were seen by most loggers as inferior to the Caterpillar brand of tractors, but their balance and power made them way better on steep shows like this one.

Art Marshall was a funny-looking guy with a receding chin and forehead, and if you didn't know him, you would be inclined to wonder if he had the full deck. You would never think he was a university graduate and a very smart man. My dad used to play card games with him, and he said that Art could remember every card played. I used to talk with him for hours when we lived there, and I learned he had a master plan and a goal for his life. He said he only needed to work for a few more years, and then he was going to buy a house in the rich Shaughnessy district of Vancouver and play golf the rest of his life. He said he had almost a million dollars in second mortgages, and at 12 percent his money was doubling every eight years, and as soon as he was worth a million, he was off. And, you know, that is exactly what he did. I talked with a guy who'd gone to school with Art's wife, Frances, and still kept in touch, and he said that Art had repossessed a small house in the Shaughnessy district, joined the exclusive golf club and played golf as much as he wanted. When I last saw him, he only had a couple of years more to put in on his sentence on the "Rock" as he called Nelson Island. Some people who would rather live someplace else think of it as a prison sentence.

Art had never levelled his house when he moved it to Milligan's Beach, and it had no bathroom, so I had to do a bit of work before my wife, Doris, and our three kids could move in for the summer of 1961. We had a propane stove, a kerosene fridge, bed frames and a little furniture, so we got by. But the floor was a checkerboard of foot-square red and white tiles, and with it being slanted too, our little girl, Martina, was so confused that she just sat in the middle of the floor and cried. After I borrowed a Gilchrist jack and jacked the low side up level, Martina was okay again. The house wasn't too bad when we were finished fixing it up, and we put in a nice summer there. Ocean Lake Estates on West Lake had a long float that led up to the store and laundromat and showers that were run by a couple, Hazen and Merilou Young. (Her parents lived in Ballet Bay inside Blind Bay.) For a treat Doris and I would take the kids for a picnic on the nice sandy beach on the lake, get a few fresh supplies and ice cream cones and go home.

Lew Milligan and his wife, Joan, lived not far from us out toward the point. Lew had brought his outfit to Vanguard in 1949 to log until the timber was gone, and he had started out living in a temporary shelter on the beach then built the beautiful house you can still see today. In the 1950s he did jobs for Hydro when they needed mountain roads built in very challenging places, and then they called on Lew and his boys to get the towers in for the Jervis Inlet crossing. He logged off the whole mountainside just north of Beaver or Treat Creek, and you can still make out the steep switchbacks in the road from the beach nearly to the top of the mountain. Later he ran a barge-dumping and log-sorting grounds in Vanguard Bay and a few other places in the inlet as well. In fact, he just might win the prize for the most working years spent in Jervis Inlet.

I revisited the Milligan place in Vanguard Bay in 2011 and found Lew's son, Doug, and his wife happily retired there in a newly rebuilt house; his sister Sue has a place in nearby Telescope Pass. Doug graciously agreed to write his memories of his dad's logging career in Jervis Inlet.

LOGGING IN JERVIS INLET

by Doug Milligan

Lewis and Joan Milligan moved into Vanguard Bay on Nelson Island in the summer of 1949. At that time they had three years' supply of wood, but additional timber purchases on Nelson Island and at Beaver Creek in Jervis Inlet and eventually the log-sorting operations kept him busy for the next forty years.

In the beginning Lew and his cousin John formed L&J Timber. They had a D7 Cat and arch to build logging roads and Cat-log their first timber. They constructed their culverts and bridges out of cedar slab planks and logs and covered them with gravel, and they lasted well into the 1990s. As the lower-elevation timber ran out, they extended truck roads to the top of the mountain and along the ridge; in some areas these roads were 30 percent grade. Then Lew converted two six-wheel tank retrievers into logging trucks and installed four-hundred-gallon pressurized water tanks to cool the brakes on the way down.

Joan and Lewis Milligan. Lew logged, built roads for BC Hydro and ran a barge-dumping and log-sorting grounds. COURTESY DOUG MILLIGAN

Truck logging on extremely steep grades is hazardous, and steering those six-wheel-drive trucks was hard work. Power steering had been installed on their Mack trucks, and it tore the

The Haida Monarch *before a log dump.* COURTESY DOUG MILLIGAN

ball joints and tie rods apart, and when one wheel had more traction than the other, the brakes on the front wheels caused the steering wheel to spin. Lew's solution was to disconnect the power steering and the front brakes. Before the trucks started down the last steep hills into the camp, the procedure was to stop on the last flat, check the pressure and water flow to the brakes and the brake pressure balance then shift into bull low. One morning when they were working the early shift, the driver forgot to stop and check and as a result had a runaway, and it went off the road into the canyon. The truck was a write-off, but the driver jumped and only broke his leg.

In the mid-1950s Lew got contracts to clear the power line right-of-way across Nelson Island, construct an access road to the tower site for the power line span to the mainland and house the power line contractor's crew. At the same time he was logging two sides on the top of the island. In order to house all these men, he purchased Gustavson Brothers' abandoned logging camp at Deserted Bay and moved it down the inlet on huge log rafts, which were towed by the camp boat *Vanguard* and George Larson's fishboat *Wander Bird*. The road, much of which had to be blasted out of solid granite, had to be constructed in the winter, but there was a great deal of snow that year and in order to keep the job moving, Lew set up a small camp near the worksite on top of the mountain. As the cold weather continued, all logging and the clearing of the right-of-way came to a stop, but the road-building continued and as the water that seeped down the road froze, such a thick layer of ice built up that even the TD24 Cat was unable to claw its way up. The only vehicle that could get up to the road camp was a Willys jeep with chains on all four wheels.

Lewis owned an International TD18, which he had used both Cat-logging and road-building. On the Cat show in Blind Bay, he yarded and hauled with an arch that followed behind the Cat to hold the ends of the logs up off the ground. But on steep ground an arch is often in the way and at times turns over, causing delays while it is put back on its feet, so one of his innovations was to cut the fairleads off the arch and erect them on a frame over the drum

The Haida Monarch *finishes a log dump.* COURTESY DOUG MILLIGAN

The kids' school boat, the White Wing. *Barrie Farrell of Pender Harbour built it.* COURTESY DOUG MILLIGAN

of the Cat. This system worked so well that this type of rig began to be manufactured commercially.

When the C-frame on the TD18 cracked, the manufacturer told Lew that it could not be welded and would require an expensive replacement. He had heard this kind of stuff before, but he was a trained welder and had made numerous impossible welding repairs. So he welded that C-frame, and it was still holding together years later. In the early 1960s he moved the camp from Vanguard Bay to Beaver (Treat) Creek, just across from Andy Olson's camp, and built a switchback road halfway up the mountain on the left side of the creek. This time, rather than try to use trucks, he logged with Le Tourneau Electric Arches. These huge machines had tires nearly twice the height of a man, and they were driven by electric motors in huge planetary drives. As they were articulated, they were very manoeuvrable and could drag as much wood as a logging truck could over a lot steeper terrain. The Electric Arch could move a lot of logs on those steep roads, but in wet weather the roads became a river of mud. During one very wet period the machine arrived at the beach with a turn of logs, followed by a wall of mud and rock that had been the roadbed minutes before.

At the donkey setting, the yarding crew had made up turns for the Electric Arch to speed up turn-around time. On one occasion Lew was standing off to the side when a big log fell off the top of the turn and dropped onto a cedar log hanging in the chocker below. A slab blew off the cedar and hit Lewis in the face. The crew rushed him to St Mary's Hospital in Pender Harbour where the doctor patched him up. His jaw was broken, his dentures were smashed, and the remains of his glasses had to be picked out of his face, piece by piece. But he refused to stay in the hospital and was back in camp two days later. Since there was no radio in camp, the first Joan knew of the accident was when Lew arrived home, bandaged and bruised, looking for his spare glasses.

Once a problem black bear started prowling around the cookhouse, which had a pantry behind the kitchen with a separate outside door. The walk-in freezer was a structure with its own door fitted into the back of the pantry. The bear attempted to tear the wall off the freezer from the outside without success, so he smashed the pantry door and tried to tear the freezer door off from inside the pantry. By the time the bear broke into the pantry, the whole camp was awake, and someone was pounding on Andy Olson's door in the next camp. Andy hunted cougars and had the only rifle around. The bear did a lot of damage, but the freezer door held, and Andy's marksmanship saved the grub for another day. (The Olson brothers logged the mountainside above where the Kleins and Campbell had logged in 1937, and where Delta Rock later mined–and still mines–gravel.)

Freight delivery for the camp, especially for heavy items, presented challenges. Once, when a spool of cable was delivered by freight boat, it arrived as usual when no one was at camp. The cable was offloaded onto the stiff-leg, which was made up of three big fir logs lashed together. As the tide dropped, the stiff-leg tilted and the spool rolled overboard. A diver went down and found the spool sitting on end; had it landed on its side, it would have rolled into the depths of Jervis Inlet, never to be seen again. As it was, the diver connected a cable from the Electric Arch, and they dragged it ashore with no serious damage, just another unplanned expense.

While Lew was logging at Beaver Creek, he travelled back and

The Vanguard, *one of the old logging camp boats.* COURTESY DOUG MILLIGAN

forth to Vanguard Bay to check on his family. During the daytime, this is an easy twelve-mile run, but on those wet and windy and often foggy nights, it required very competent dead-reckoning skills, especially when your navigation equipment was a compass, a watch and a searchlight. Somehow he always made it home. Years later he took a power squadron boating course, and strangely, the navigation section was a problem for him, even though his self-taught system had served him well for all those years.

In the late 1960s Lew switched from logging to log sorting with grounds first in Vanguard Bay and later relocated to St. Vincent Bay and Annis Bay. He retired in the mid-1980s.

Saltery Bay

Saltery Bay on the Powell River side of Jervis Inlet became one of the favourite places for the people from Blind Bay to settle so they could be closer to schools and other facilities. I guess they could still look across and see the familiar mountains and Hardy Island, and some of them still had property over there. It is at the south end of the Powell River road to Vancouver, where the ferry takes about fifty minutes to Earls Cove. There are two sets of transmission lines nearby that carry power across Jervis Inlet to the mills and the people of the whole area, and one of them had the longest power line span in the world when it was first put across Jervis Inlet. Close to the provincial campgrounds there is a midden that is part of the abandoned First Nations village of Skuhlp, proving that there was a First Nations dependence and presence on this creek in pre-European occupation times.

The bay got its name from a Japanese salmon saltery that sat on pilings there in the early years of the twentieth century, but the last owner was a guy named McNair. At that time there must have been a good-sized run of chum or dog salmon coming back to the many creeks in Jervis Inlet, and they would have supplied the saltery. (When chum salmon are spawning, the males fight a lot and grow large teeth that look like dogs' teeth.)

An old retired logger named Frank Jenkinson lived near the creek at Saltery Bay, and after he made himself sort of a caretaker of the salmon, he learned something that the scientists at the Department of Fisheries and Oceans didn't know. The salmon spawn in the fall when the storms sweep in and drop their load of rain, raising water levels higher than normal. That's when the salmon dig their redds, but when the water level goes down, the eggs are left high and dry. It was thought that these eggs were lost without water to keep them supplied with oxygen, but old Frank discovered that, even if the gravel was only wet, the alevins were still alive, getting nourishment from the egg sack while they were growing down there in the gravel. This is the way it is supposed to work. After the egg sack has been absorbed, in a matter of a few days all these little fish wiggle their way up through the gravel and out into the creek and estuary where they grow and feed for some time until they are ready to start following the coastline out to the North Pacific feeding grounds. By channelling water to these dried-out areas in the creek bed, Frank could take his shovel and gently tease these little fish out and into the stream. In some places they were so thick he would have a hundred or more in one shovelful. But the timing is critical as the little fish have to have absorbed all the egg sack and be able to live on their own, and it required someone willing to take the time to do it right. Frank Jenkinson brought this little creek back from very low numbers, and in their salmon enhancement brochures the DFO called him "the man who digs for salmon." Jenkinson Road in Saltery Bay is named in his memory.

The Other Pioneers of Nelson Island

Karen Southern did a pretty good job documenting the pioneers who lived in the coves and bays of Nelson Island in her book, *The Nelson Island Story* (Hancock House, 1987), but she missed a few good stories. She mentions a poor farmer named John Baggs living in a meadow beside a creek that runs into Baggs' Bay, the next bay west of Quarry Bay. My Uncle Charlie Sundquist lived with Baggs and his many children for a few weeks—I'm not sure of the date, but I would guess it would have been before Charlie joined the Royal Canadian Navy in World War I. Baggs was eking out a poor living from his ranch, but he had quite a few fruit trees, a big garden, a cow or two and a big sow pig with about ten weaner pigs. Charlie had the job of feeding the pigs, so he knew how many there were. One day Baggs said he was going to kill one of his pigs, and if Charlie would go hunt a deer, they would have enough meat for a while. That night when Charlie packed in a nice deer, he found a beautiful pork dinner waiting for him. Next day he went out to feed the pigs and there were none missing, so he finally had to ask old Baggs where he got the pig. Baggs admitted he fooled Charlie by cooking a big porcupine that he had trapped, but Charlie said it was as good as any pork he had ever eaten.

In 1945 my dad and I went in to have a look at Baggs' orchard, and the meadow was still free of brush and most of the fruit trees were still alive. Quite close to the meadow on the water side there was an old log skidway called a "roader" that at one time was lined with small logs to keep the logs in the ditch. A big winch held a mile or more of small main-line cable with a lighter haulback to pull the rigging back for another load. There were a number of rollers cut into stumps to keep the lines in place.

At the north end of Agamemnon Channel, at the extreme end of Nelson Island, there is a little island with a spit joining it to Nile Point that is only covered at high tide. The local name was Sawmill Bay because a man named Jorgenson and his family used to operate a sawmill there. He eventually quit and went on to have a logging operation up Jervis for many years. When he retired, he bought the old relief camp at Wood Bay, where he set up a good mill and moved a lot of machines in for storage. One huge yarding machine had come from California where it worked in the redwood forest. After Jorgenson died, Andy Sterloff acquired the property.

Life on Alcatraz Island

Jim Read lived on Caldwell Island in Agamemnon Channel for many years with his wife, Lou, and his only son, George. If you asked him where he lived, he would say he lived on Alcatraz, so for years I didn't know it had any other name. Jim was a wiry guy about six feet four inches tall. He and Lou, who was about five feet tall, did everything together, even logging with a little gas donkey on a float and a small A-frame. Lou ran the machine while Jim did the rest. For years they lived and worked in the area then bought the island and built a small house on it. Then along came George. As he grew up, he learned how to do things with his dad. They built a bigger house, landscaped gardens and even built boats together. He must have done school by correspondence as they were miles from the nearest school. As George grew to manhood, he was as tall as his dad. The whole family worked together handlogging, log salvaging or yarding logs with the little machine. Jim would get a mile of timber claim at a time in Agamemnon Channel, and even though it was a handlogging claim where you couldn't use power, the Forest Service would allow him to use power on some designated parts. One day I was talking to Bill Brown, the assistant ranger, about getting a handlogging claim at a small lake by our claim, and somehow the conversation got around to Jim Read's claim in Boom Bay, and how far up the mountain he was handlogging his timber. Bill said Jim was the only man who had a yellow cedar log in a handlog boom. When Bill questioned Jim about how this was possible, since yellow cedar doesn't grow below two thousand feet in this area, Jim swore he could show him the stump. Brown declined the offer when he looked at the hill he would have to climb in order to charge him with taking a log that was floating by.

Jim and Lou's world shattered when George's fourteen-foot boat that he had built himself was found floating a mile or so from home. He'd been going to Irvines Landing to pick up his mom and dad from a trip to Vancouver. George, for all his life on the water, had never learned to swim, and after stopping the boat to adjust something, he must have fallen overboard and couldn't get back in the boat. George's body was never found. Jim and Lou sold the island and moved to Vancouver in 1976. For many years after the Reads left, Fielding's log barge dumping and sorting grounds used Caldwell Island and part of Westmere Bay.

Westmere

West Lake is the biggest lake on Nelson Island and reaches from Westmere Bay on Agamemnon Channel and nearly meets the salt water at the head of Vanguard Bay. At Westmere a short road beside the lake's only outlet creek rises about twenty or thirty feet above sea level to this beautiful lake. At about half tide the remains of a First Nations fish trap can be seen across the mouth of the creek. Trout have been caught up to five pounds in the lake, and I have heard there were coho salmon there in good numbers in the past as well as some chum and sockeye.

John and George West and their mother came to Nelson Island at the turn of the century after a short time in Pender Harbour as the proprietors of the Irvines Landing facilities, and they acquired property beside the creek that leads out of West Lake. Against the advice of a lot of naysayers who reminded him that Irvines Landing was only a few miles away, John West began to build a seventeen-room hotel with a store and post office. But his advisers were right. There was not enough business to sustain it, and rather than try to keep the huge building warm, he cut it in half and burned the lumber from one half in the stove of the other half. The irony is that many years later when Laurie Wray took over the hotel and needed more room for his guests, he had to build an addition onto the old building. Old John was just ahead of time. After his failed attempt at the hotel, John worked at logging. He married a bride from England and soon had a family, starting with John Jr. in 1913, then Pansy and Robin. After a logging career involving a steam donkey operation, John Sr. died in the 1940s. John Jr. was still living in his own home at Egmont at the time of his death in 2012. John Sr.'s brother, George, built at West Lake and took their mother to live there. His overturned canoe was found drifting in the lake, and it was assumed he fell out and drowned.

The Green Bay Area

Below Westmere Bay, halfway to the point of Green Bay, there is a mariculture lease that used to be owned by the Campbell family, one of the first fish farms in the Jervis Inlet area. A series of plankton blooms killed their fish in the early 1990s, and the Campbell family was wiped out, as were many others. They switched their leases to oysters, sold out and moved away. When I was thirteen, my dad and Uncle Pete had built a little house on the lower point of this property to live in while they logged a setting on the hill above. My job was pulling all the nails out of the used lumber they salvaged from an old house. After we moved in, they began to build a four-hundred-foot log chute to get the coldeck pile into the chuck. My career as a logger started at this spot; I was the signalman. My next memory of Green Bay was when my dad took me to Frank White's camp. The only thing that impressed me was how wet the beach area was from the spray coming from the falls, and the truck that Frank had put two motors in to get enough power. The dealer for Mack Trucks, Charlie Philp, was involved, so I would guess this one-of-a-kind, two-engined truck was used in the beginning.

In 1957 I was contract falling and bucking for Dubois

Logging over in the watershed at the head of Quarry Lake. We had built a road from the end of Frank White's road up over the hill and down to the lake, and to get to work, we took the crew boat to Green Bay and an old jeep pickup from the beach up the old logging road. But one morning when it had frozen the night before, the old jeep took a long time to warm up enough to make it up the first hill. Raleigh Heid was the boss as well as the driver. I sat in the middle, and Babe Kammerle was next to the door, and Bob H. Lee, Ben Dubois and Ed Crocker were in the back. The brakes were low on fluid and needed to be pumped to work at all. Raleigh was impatient and decided to try the hill too soon and it stalled out, so he flipped it into reverse in the low range and reversed it down to the flat where he tried again. This time he made it up around the corner above the falls before the engine stalled, only this time he missed the gear, and away we went backwards straight for the falls. As soon as it stopped moving ahead, the guys in the back jumped off. I tried to get Babe to open the door, but he was afraid the door would get him. Raleigh was gripping the wheel and pumping the brakes, and we were picking up speed straight for the falls, a sheer drop of fifty feet onto the beach. I could see that the only hope was to turn to avoid going over the falls, so I braced myself, pulled the wheel out of Raleigh's hands and turned the truck partly back the way we had come. I was hoping to hit a big rock that was on the top side of the road, but we were going too fast, and the front wheel fell off the bridge. We slid the full length of the bridge with the belly dragging on the gravel, which brought us to a gentle stop.

After a half hour with ropes and pry bars, we had the truck back on the road with not a scratch on the old girl. It was suggested that we should stop everything and try to find out why it was so gutless, but the boss said we had wasted too much time on it already, and since it was running, we should leave well enough alone. When we got to the job, I was falling and bucking close by, so when they were all out of sight, I lifted the hood and after trying everything, I found the locking bolt on the distributor was loose. I went to my power saw tool kit and found the right-sized wrench, turned the motor on and adjusted the distributor to the highest idle, then backed it off a little, tightened the lock bolt and that was it. The next morning it just roared up that hill, and Raleigh couldn't figure out where all the power came from. It was just that the timing was late so it couldn't fire properly.

Mrs. Henry's Timber

Howard White wrote a humorous story titled "The Bomb that Mooed" that was published in *Raincoast Chronicles* about Mrs. Henry's cow eating some old dynamite. He described Mrs. Henry and her old country ways very accurately, but I experienced another side of her when my partner and I were purchasing the timber on the two-hundred-acre property she was left with on Nelson Island after her husband died. I don't know where the name Henry came from, but that is what everyone called them. His real name was Captain Ott Heikinnen (someone told me it is Finnish for Henry), and he had been a real captain in the old country in his early years. They were part of a Finnish community at some time before moving to Billings Bay in Hidden Basin and starting the Hidden Bay Farm Resort. They operated for years until the Captain got arguing with his neighbours, and then he moved the lodge and everything to the property that had been a fish cannery and later a shingle mill at the mouth of the lagoon a half mile south of Green Bay. They kept the same name and catered to their Finnish clientele, mostly from the Lower Mainland. The Captain would pick up his guests at Irvines Landing in this funny-looking little boat that he had built himself from some Old World pattern. Mrs. Henry did all the cooking and had a large garden where she grew most of the vegetables for the kitchen. They fixed up some of the mill houses for renting to people who wanted to stay awhile on their own.

The Captain began building a big funny-looking boat and hired Fred Crosby, a boat builder from Pender Harbour, to help him finish it. This was the dream boat that he intended to cruise the Coast in, and he even talked of sailing it to Finland when he retired someday. It was called *Esto Utopia* for their two names, Esther and Ott. It had a high pilot house with only a few small windows on the front. Fred Crosby told me that he had to put some new ribs in because it had sat around so many years that the old ribs were rotting and had to be replaced. The originals were big limbs sawn in half so they could be bent. Perhaps the Captain had run short of the good bending oak and substituted. Outside of this problem, the workmanship and material were good. It was launched and made a few short runs before the old Captain's death. I saw it out on the fishing grounds in the late 1960s. The new owner had taken the back cabin off, put on a deck, a fish hold and some windows, and it looked a lot better.

After the Captain died, Mrs. Henry was too old to carry on by herself. She was getting ready to move away someday in the not too distant future, but to get the most out of their property, she wanted to sell the timber first. We were looking for more timber and went up one day to see what kind of a deal we could do. She invited us in, and it soon became obvious that she had done her homework and was a pretty good businesswoman. Our estimate of her trees was close to what she had been told by others, so we were off to a good start. She seemed to be worried that there could be more than expected, so we offered a fixed amount based on a certain cut, and after that was reached, so much per thousand board feet. She liked the deal and gave us sixty days to come up with the first part. We had been dealing with a sawmill called Anderson Brothers and were able to get a loan from them for the payment with a first refusal of the logs to repay the loan. Oliver Dubois had his eye on this same timber for some time, but he had been hoping to wait until the old girl was a bit desperate to get a bargain price. Our offer fouled up his plan, so he put pressure on his broker to have our money cut off, which is what happened because his broker was related by marriage to the mill owner. Now we only had two weeks left on our agreement. We went back and told Mrs. Henry what was going on, and she said Dubois had come and offered her more money, but she was from the old school and didn't like those tactics, so she gave us more time. We changed brokers, and he loaned us the money. She allowed us to dump in the lagoon not far from her house and even gave us vegetables to take home from her garden. The claim produced above what we estimated, so she got some more money afterward. It wasn't too long after that she sold the place to the Viitenen family, one of her old guests. They lived there for years trying to make a living growing orchids for the market.

Earls Cove

It seems that Charles Roscoe Johnstone, who came up from the US about 1902, may have been the first white man to live in Earls Cove on the east side of Agamemnon Channel. He and his wife, Dora, bought a big sailboat in Seattle and sailed upcoast until they reached the Jervis Inlet area and built a small shake house on the beach at Earls Cove. One of their sons was born there, but afterwards they moved further up Jervis to Vancouver Bay. It may have been the Johnstones' shake house that the family of Martha Rouse (later Warnock) moved into about 1909.

In those early years there was a logging railway from Earls Cove into Ruby Lake, and it must have been a sizable operation because before the outfit went broke they had filled the lake with logs. Since the Sunshine Coast Highway was finished to Earls Cove, there have been many attempts to salvage these sunken logs with some success, and even after all these years underwater they are still sound.

Some time after World War I, the Earl family arrived and built the big house that is still standing on the hill behind the restaurant. They put in an orchard and a big garden. I don't know what the father, Tom Earl, did for a living at that time, but when I knew the three boys—Leslie, Norman and Tommy—and their mother, the boys were salmon trollers, and they would leave their mother there for the summer while they went north fishing. The father had died by his own hand when the boys were in their teens. He was a strange man and would shoot at boats that tried to come too close. They say he was shell-shocked in the war; nowadays they call it post-traumatic stress disorder, and you can get psychiatric therapy and help.

One day when I was talking to Norman, he seemed to want to talk about his dad's death. He was still angry with him for the way he planned it and caused so much pain to his family. He had taken the two oldest boys, Les and Norman, up on the hill behind the house to fall a big fir for firewood. He helped them chop the undercut and started the back cut, then he told them to finish it while he went back to the house. Instead he stood right where the tree was going to fall, and that's where they found him. According to Norman, it was not a pretty sight. He was still alive, but due to the weather, they were unable to get him to the hospital in time to save his life.

Earls Cove was the end of the road to Vancouver so that's where the BC Ferry terminal was built. When we were starting to clear the hundred-foot-wide right-of-way from Kleindale, Old John Cline (also known as John Klein), the main right-of-way contractor, started us out with instructions on what to do in the clearing job. The last thing he said was "Away you go, and don't stop till you come to Earl's apple trees." I wonder what old man Earl would have to say about all the strangers going through his garden today.

Some Residents of Agamemnon Channel and Bay

Across from Read's Caldwell Island in a little bay with a small island in it, right where the creek from Ambrose Lake dumps into the channel, lived an old man that the locals called "Pink Whiskers." He used mercurochrome, which stained his big white beard. I never did hear his real name. A little further up the channel, just below the Native pictograph site, a fisherman named George Day lived in a small house, and he had his float in the channel just below the bluff.

The Earls' place was just north of the same bluff, the next family was the Sladeys, and Olaus Lee lived in the corner of Agamemnon Bay. Peter Sladey was a gillnet fisherman and lived there most of his life. He had two sons, Vic and Ollie. I think there was a girl as well. Vic went to Vancouver to work, but Ollie followed his dad into fishing with his own boat. After he married Jean Murdock, a Pender Harbour girl, he settled in Pender and started logging in a small way with a T6 International crawler, about the smallest Cat in the woods, just half a mile west of Fearney Point in a little bay I think is called Whalebone Bay. After a while he got a bigger machine and a few employees and did very well. Eventually he built the first motel in Madeira Park and in later years branched out into real estate and developing subdivisions in the area.

I worked for Ollie blasting rock for his Cat road for a while. Most of his claims were in Jervis Inlet, where he kept his operation going with a few long-term men. Ollie's son, Doug, has followed him into the logging and subdivision business in the area and is one of the biggest logging contractors in the Jervis Inlet area, employing a lot of Pender and Egmont loggers at his many sites. Four generations of Peter Sladey's descendants still make their homes not far from his original Jervis Inlet home.

Olaus Lee settled in the Bay with his wife and four kids, but he went north to Rivers and Smith inlets for the gillnet season every year for the rest of his life. When the last girl, Nancy, was about five, Mrs. Lee died of a kidney disease. Olaus was left with four kids to raise, so he sold the forty-acre property now called Moccasin Valley to Herman Boutilier and rented a big house in Garden Bay. When he was away fishing, the oldest three could look after themselves, but he boarded little Nancy with Bill and Elsie Klein. He lived at Garden Bay until all the kids left home, and some years later passed away on the fishing grounds, leaving his son Robert to run his boat, the *Tom Boy*, back to Pender Harbour. Olaus Lee built a lot of houses and boats when he was not fishing; he built part of my house, too.

A Fishing Holiday

Sometimes Dad got tired of logging and rigged up his boat to fish, and when I was about thirteen, he took me with him for a few weeks. The boat was an old Columbia River gillnet sailboat that had been converted to a gas engine—a four-cylinder "Star" car engine. Two of the pistons had been removed to save fuel, so it only did about six knots. The boat was only twenty-eight feet long with an eight-foot beam. The fish hold had wooden plugs that could be removed to flood the hold for live tanks. Dad had built a longline drum called a "Christmas tree" that stood on end with pre-baited hooks on two-foot leaders called gangings hanging down. One man baited the hooks for the next set as the gear was hauled and the fish taken off. It worked so well we even caught someone's dog that was helping himself to our bait when we were delivering our fish. He got hooked through the lip, and we had some time getting it out after we cut him free.

We longlined for bottom fish all around Nelson Island and lower Jervis Inlet, and Dad always tried to stop and visit some old-timer living by himself in some bay or other. One that I remember was an old troller named Tug Wilson that Dad had known since his first years in Jervis. He had a strange English accent and had served in the British army in Africa and India before he pre-empted property in Agamemnon Bay in 1912 with another buddy named Youngblundt, whose niece, Nelly, married Tom Earl of Earls Cove. Man, how that Wilson guy could talk and give advice where the best fishing spots were. He tried to convince Dad to go to "Agaminion Buy," as he pronounced it, as it was the best place to catch spring salmon at that time of year, but he didn't seem to be in a hurry to go there himself, and neither did we.

Another old guy we visited was Tom Brazil on Hardy Island. Dad had known him for many years, so we stayed overnight and had a real good visit. He put on a real show for me with his tame deer and pheasants. He sure seemed to appreciate our visit. We also visited old Pete Day who had been partners with Dad and Tom Robinson in the early years

The store on the north shore of Egmont. We sold our red cod there for three cents a pound. COURTESY BEA SWANSON

when they horse logged together at Elephant Point on the west side of Hotham Sound. He was still living in the house right next to where Dad had lived when he lived in St. Vincent Bay. We also talked to Jack Williams, their only other neighbour in St. Vincent Bay. He had a mink ranch near the little bay where Gus Angus has his fish farm now. Jack had to fish every day with longlines to keep his mink fed, and you could smell those mink pens as you were going by in the boat. When we were through all our visiting, we had to go to Egmont to sell our fish, and I remember we got three cents a pound for our red cod.

Picking Oysters in Jervis Inlet

My dad had told me about the small native oysters that were in Hotham Sound when he first arrived in 1919, though they were few and far between even then. About that time Ian McKechnie, the guy who ran the shingle mill at Green Bay, moved to Pender Harbour, and his dad, who was a doctor, imported some of the big, fast-growing Pacific or Japanese oysters for him to grow in these waters. My Uncle Bill Klein also got some of the seed and put them on beds in front of his property in Kleindale right across from McKechnie's place. Uncle Bill kept going until he was able to ship oysters to Vancouver on the Union boat and make a living at it.

When the sea water temperature reaches close to seventy degrees Fahrenheit, the oysters begin to spawn, and after they hatch, the oysters are free floating and feed on plankton as they drift with the tides. After a couple of weeks they attach to the beach in the intertidal zone and grow until they are mature enough in a few years to spawn themselves. In a matter of a few cycles the little oysters made it from Pender Harbour to Agamemnon Channel and eventually to every bay and inlet in the Jervis Inlet system.

When I was fifteen, I worked for Uncle Bill in his shucking house and learned how to shuck oysters the right way. Not long after this, the Western Fish Company started to pay $4.50 per gallon of oysters, and they supplied the new one-gallon cans for free. My dad was out of work and decided to try the oyster business, so, armed with a couple of oyster knives, we got a dozen cans from Gill Mervin, the fish buyer, and went up Agamemnon Channel. After finding a suitable beach, we went ashore on the falling tide, and as soon as the highest oysters appeared, we went to work until the rising tide chased us off three or four hours later. Dad had never shucked oysters before, except a few to eat, so I showed him what Uncle Bill had taught me, and he caught on fast. We wore gloves and used short planks to open the oysters to avoid dulling the knives on the rocks. You hold the oyster on the plank firmly with your left hand, with the flat side up and the heel towards your belly, so the muscle you have to cut is always close to the right side of the shell. Push hard, and wiggle the knife between the upper and lower halves. As soon as the knife is in, you gently push it then swing it back and forth to cut the muscle and pry the top shell off, making sure that the muscle is cut cleanly from the shell but still attached to the oyster body. The black mantle should be intact. When cutting the muscle loose, it is best to only pry the top shell open an inch, reach your knife in from the front and cut very close to the shell. Your knife blade should be at least three inches long with a very thin smooth sharp blade to cut cleanly.

Uncle Bill said that if the oysters were undamaged they could live in their own juice for a week, but we had to deliver no more than three-day-old oysters. We shucked them right off the beach into the cans, so we had to make sure there was a minimum of broken shell that got in because they never got washed until they were processed in Vancouver. Dad and I could each get a gallon per hour, and since a chokerman was just making a dollar an hour in the woods at that time, we were doing okay. And sometimes we would take a gunnysack-full back to the boat to work on later.

Once we found a beach just loaded with perfect-looking oysters at the head of Hotham Sound. We could see them underwater. Uncle Charlie Sundquist had just come back from the merchant marine and needed a job, so we decided to tow an old boat hull that Dad owned up to Hotham to get a load of these oysters. Hector McCall had a nice troller called the *Four Freedoms*, and we talked him into the deal. We left in time to make the low tide, which was in the middle of the night, and put about four tons of oysters into the old hull and sacks full into the troller and headed back to the Harbour. The next day we all showed up to start shucking, but after the first dozen we discovered what a huge mistake we'd made. The oysters were so thin that you could see right through them. We hadn't opened one up to that point to check for quality. With the oysters growing so close together at the end of Hotham where the water circulation was so poor, they weren't getting enough plankton, and they were all close to starvation. It was a case of very bad planning on our part. We scattered them along the beach on Forester's oyster lease just across the bay from Uncle Bill's place, so maybe when they fattened up he was able to use them.

Henry Harris and his wife, Sis, were life-long residents of Jervis Inlet and when they retired from logging they bought a gillnet vessel, the *Derald H*, and started fishing the coast for salmon. The salmon season was only three months, so they looked for something to do for the winter months and tried fishing black cod, digging clams and beachcombing for logs, all with some success. Then they noticed all the oysters on the beaches and looked for a way to take advantage of this seemingly endless resource. They bought the property in St. Vincent Bay where Gus Angus has his fish farm and built a shucking house. Then they hit a snag: they had to get it approved by the DFO. It seemed there was a lot of foot-dragging on the part of the officials before they were allowed to sell one oyster. Even the fresh water that flowed in the little stream past their shucking house was deemed unsafe to wash the oysters in, and they were told they needed a fortune in filters. But they stuck with the process until they finally got their licence. How different from when we only needed a personal fishing licence to do the same thing.

The Silveys of Egmont

Reggie and Charlie, Dad's younger brothers, lived in Egmont, but there was no road to Egmont as there is now so they didn't see one another for long stretches. One of the first non-Native men, if not the first, to live in Egmont was Portuguese Joe Silvey, who fished Jervis Inlet from 1872 to the late 1890s, and during this time he built a big saltery on property that has been occupied by the Silvey family ever since. It is also recorded that John Wray lived there with his large family before he homesteaded at Fearny Point. The Griffith family, the Vaughns and the Jefferies also had a part in the early community. In 1915 P.B. Anderson moved in with his railroad camp from Pender Harbour, running rails from Waugh Lake and the Skookumchuck and dumping his logs into what is locally called Co-op Bay. By the time my dad's family arrived in 1920, there was a store and fish-buying station at Egmont and, I believe, a post office as well. You can still find those old pioneers' names among the present population, though many have moved away to Sechelt and other places.

A lot of my friends and some relatives claim to be related to Portuguese Joe Silvey and his second wife, Kwatleemaht

(Lucy) Silvey, so I felt that any story of Jervis Inlet should include this amazing man's adventures. Realizing that in most versions of his story there are difficulties with old country and church records, birth and marriage dates, I went to Barbara Higgins, who was born and raised in Egmont and knew most of the characters.

I have known Barbara and Richard Higgins for forty-five years. After she moved from the Sunshine Coast to go to university in Victoria, she became a teacher and taught in the far north of Canada. Since retiring to Sechelt, she has taken her place as an elder of the governing body of the Sechelt Nation, and at eighty-plus is still going strong. She has graciously allowed me to use a portion from a future book.

PORTUGUESE JOE SILVEY, AKA PORTUGUESE JOE #1 (BIRTH NAME: JOSEPH SIMMONS).

Researched and written by his great-granddaughter, X̲wu'p'a'lich, Barbara Higgins

My grandfather, Henry Silvey of Egmont, BC, and I used to sit on his wharf or float for hours on end as he told me stories about his father and about life on Kuper Island before he moved to Egmont. He often lamented that his sons and daughters showed no interest in their Portuguese roots. He was aware that my maternal grandparents were relating all the Sechelt tales to me, and he wanted to make sure that I took notice of my Portuguese heritage as well.

According to my grandfather, his father was born on Pico Island, Azores, Portugal, to Francesca Hyacynthia Sylvia or Silvy or Silvey and a Scotsman named John Simmons, a medium-high ranking soldier who had travelled to Portugal to fight in one of the many wars. He owned a whaling schooner, and when the war was over, he stayed in Portugal to win the hand of the beautiful Francesca Hyacynthia Sylvia. My grandfather Henry said with much pride, "My grandfather, John Simmons, travelled the seven seas to wherever there was profit to be earned. He was a top-notch whaler and an excellent soldier."

John Simmons and Francesca Silvey were blessed with two sons, Manuel and Joseph, and in the old whaling tradition, when Manuel reached twelve years, he became the cabin boy aboard his father's schooner, which was called the *Morning Star*. He was two years older than Joe, and very proud to take his position there. He fished with his father for a couple of years, but when they were hunting whales off the east coast of North America, Manuel became ill and died. Joseph was devastated at the loss of the brother he loved so dearly. Grandpa said the family grieved, but they had to get on with life and put the loss of Manuel behind them. So when the *Morning Star* made its next trip back to Pico Island, Joe, who was now twelve years old, joined the crew as his father's new cabin boy.

Joe had a mind of his own and he didn't stay with whaling very long. After sailing around Cape Horn, in the tradition of all sailors who lived through the experience, he had his left ear pierced and a gold earring inserted. "He wore it with pride," Grandpa said. It is unclear why he left his father's ship; he was only around fifteen years old when he took part in the tail-end of the California gold rush, which occurred between 1849 and 1855. But he was not lucky in his search for gold, and he returned to his father's schooner, which was now fishing on the west coast on North America. They travelled north to Vancouver Island where the ship was involved in a serious accident, and when they went into Fort Victoria for repairs, he left the ship.

He worked around Victoria for a few months until the weather cleared up, then he outfitted a huge Indian canoe, took on five Portuguese sailors and headed for Point Roberts where he started a trading post, trading with fishermen and Indian people. When he heard about gold being discovered on Indian land at Yale, he was bitten by the gold-fever bug again, and he and his Portuguese sailors set sail for Yale. He thought he would have no problem as he had traded with the Indians of many villages without incident, but Joe and his friends hardly got started gold seeking before the Yale Indians began killing off the would-be miners. He barely escaped with his life when they burned his house to the ground, and in the dark of the night he and his friends started down the Fraser River as fast as they could paddle. They were as quiet as they could possibly be, but the Indians found out they were on the river and pursued them in three or four canoes. They were so frightened they didn't dare stop anywhere.

According to Joe, the night was very dark and as they ploughed down the waterway they took chances in the pitch blackness of the night that they would never have considered doing in the light of day. The Indians following them seemed to have no fear of the water and took the shortest route through the turbulence, and they sang all the way with the helmsmen beating time on the sides of the canoes. With hearts wracked by fear, Joe and his friends could hear the canoes gaining on them. Finally, dog-tired and shaking with fear, they came to one of those small islands below Hope and took a big chance and went ashore. Slipping and sliding in their haste, they carried the canoe up into the trees out of sight–and the Indian canoes sped by without noticing them. They stayed still for hours, afraid the Indians would double back and discover them.

Early the next day they made their way down the river, and just when they thought they were safe, they discovered a whole tribe of Indians on the shore at Musqueam. They began praying to their God because they thought these were the same Indians that had chased them down the river. They figured they were dead men for sure. It never dawned on them that there were different tribes of Indians, and this was a different tribe who beckoned to them, inviting them to come ashore. With much trepidation they landed on the beach, and the Indians welcomed them like guests and invited them to share food with them. It turned out that this was the great Chief Kiapilano (Capilano) and his people.

From that first brief meeting they became good friends, and a few months later Portuguese Joe returned to Musqueam and asked Chief Kiapilano for the hand of his granddaughter, Kaaltinaht (Mary Ann). The chiefs officiated at a huge wedding feast to celebrate the marriage. When Joe and Kaaltinaht left Musqueam, their canoe was piled high with blankets and other gifts, and Kaaltinaht sat on top of the pile, as that was the way Indian princesses were treated when they married. They travelled to what is known today as Stanley Park and built their home at what is now called Brockton Point. Joe built the first boat in that area so that he could trade with the Indians who trusted him and held him in high esteem. (Actually, I believe the Vancouver Archives credits him with being the first commercial boat-builder in this new land.) It was a sailing sloop that he named *Morning Star* after his father's sailing schooner, although most of his trade was done with the Indians, fishermen and sailors who came ashore for that purpose. And that is how my great grandfather, Portuguese Joe Silvey, became the first merchant in what is now the City of Vancouver. He later moved to Gastown and built a saloon and trading post, which he called the Hole in the Wall; it was located in the seven hundred block of Abbott Street near Gassy Jack's Saloon.

Portuguese Joe taught the Musqueam and Squamish Indians how to weave stinging nettle fibres into very strong and serviceable gill nets, just as the people did in Portugal, and as they became adept at this, they made fish traps and herring scoops as well as nets to seine for herring. Grandpa said the herring were so plentiful that their little lips stuck out of the water sending kisses to the Creator for their being. It took twelve men to handle the herring seine properly, and it was always a combination of Indians and Portuguese helping each other, with the newcomers paying close attentions to the rituals and customs of the Indian people. Portuguese Joe rendered the herring down for their oil, which was very high grade, stored it in four-gallon sheet metal cans and transported it in his sloop to Nanaimo to sell it to the coal mines there for use on the machinery and in the pit-lamps that they used underground.

Joe and Kaaltinaht had three children. The eldest was Elizabeth, and she was the first child of European descent to be born in Gastown. Their second daughter was named Josephine and their son was named Francis, but Kaaltinaht never regained her strength after his birth, and she died early in 1872.

Now Portuguese Joe was left with a huge problem. He had three young children to be cared for. He came to Sechelt and met with Chief Naiamiten Julius of the Tsonei, who was a personal friend. Chief Julius and Charley Ptameldou brought him to the home of Andrew Kwakoil and Agatha Kreboulette. Andrew Kwakoil was the speaker or talker for

Chief Julius and Chief Tom as they didn't like speaking in front of an audience. Kwakoil had a beautiful daughter, Lucy Kwatleemaht, said to be of marrying age, but she was really just fifteen years old. By this time Portuguese Joe was thirty-six years, a good twenty-one years older than Kwatleemaht. Anyhow, with everyone showing a blind eye, this young child was married off to Portuguese Joe on September 20, 1872. He must have been a man of some means by this time because there is a lovely certificate of the Holy Sacrament of Matrimony and a nice picture taken on the day they were married. Even so, that must have been a frightening ordeal for Kwatleemaht. Now she was a wife and a stepmother of three young children, and she was leaving her home forever. And get this: that upstanding prelate of the Roman Catholic Church, Bishop Paul Durieu, O.M.I., was the man who sanctioned this joining and signed his name to the lies of that day. Indeed, back in those days, females were without any kind of human rights; they just did as they were told by some male–be it father, chief, husband, brother or clergy.

I have nothing but good to think of Kwatleemaht. I know that she taught her children to speak Shishalh, how to collect cedar roots and red cherry bark and how to weave baskets, everything that the women of Tsonei had taught her. She was a good mother to her children and her stepchildren, and when she died in August 1934 after her many years of good works, a Vancouver newspaper had this to say about her:

NATIVE DAUGHTER DIES

A native daughter of British Columbia who had resided in the province all her life, Mrs. Lucy Silvey-Watson, aged 75, of Reid Island died suddenly early this

> morning. According to advice received in Vancouver, Mrs. Silvey-Watson is survived by her husband, Joseph Watson of Reid Island, four sons, Domingo and Anthony Silvey of Reid Island and Joseph and Henry Silvey of Jervis Inlet, and three daughters, Mrs. J. Walker of Vancouver, Mrs. Buss of Egmont, B.C. and Mrs. Beale of Vancouver. Funeral arrangements will be announced later.

Portuguese Joe and his new wife, Kwatleemaht, fished in Jervis Inlet from 1872 to the late 1890s. Then Joe became the first Portuguese person in Canada to receive British citizenship, and he also got the sole fishing rights between Dodds Narrows and Sansum Narrows. My grandfather, Henry Silvey, who was born in 1888, had vivid memories of being aboard when his father was longlining for scrap fish and when he was hunting whales. He told me that his mom and dad had a huge saltery built on what is now Bill and Sarah Silvey's property in Silvey Bay, which was the name the bay was known by for many years until someone began calling it Secret Bay. It is my ambition to have it re-named Silvey Bay in honour of my great-grandfather, Portuguese Joe Silvey, and the fact that the Silvey family has lived in the area for so many years.

Grandpa Henry said there were huge cast iron pots at the saltery and huge drums, Indian woven baskets of all descriptions and a great stack of screens that were woven from bulrush leaves and saltwater reeds that were used to cover things as there were no plastic tarps in those days and canvas ones were hard to come by in this new land. There was a steam box for making repairs to ships, many fathoms of rope fashioned from inner cedar bark, and a windlass to haul in heavy loads. There were docks and wharves on both sides of the property. Portuguese Joe still had his sloop and a half interest in a sailing schooner along with a man named George Douglas. (The same Douglas family later lived in Pender Harbour.) Depending on the time of the year, they longlined for ground fish such as ratfish, skate and dogfish. Fish sold for three cents each, and coho salmon were considered too dry to eat and thrown back into the sea. They also bought fish from other longline fishermen then processed the livers for oil at the saltery and sold it to the Nanaimo Coal Mines. The carcasses of the scrap fish were rendered into a lesser grade of oil that he sold as skid grease to the many lumber mills on the north shore of Burrard Inlet.

When the whaling season was in full bloom, he hunted with George Douglas aboard their sailing schooner. Because of his years of fishing with the Portuguese whaling fleet, he knew how to make the harpoons that were triggered by gunpowder, and he taught this skill to the new breed of whalers here in the Pacific Northwest. Their base of operations was Pasley Island, which is situated between Keats and Bowen Islands. There the whale fishermen had huts for their families, and Kwatleemaht lived there with their children during the whaling season. When the men harpooned a whale, they towed it to Pasley where a windlass was used to winch it ashore. Grandpa said that sometimes it took many hours to get the huge mammal high enough on the beach to harvest its blubber, and then the entire community on Pasley worked together to produce the oil. He said the whalers' great knives were razor sharp, and their skill at reducing a whale to a stack of blubber was phenomenal.

On one of Portuguese Joe's numerous trips to Nanaimo to sell his oil, he discovered a 240-acre island called Reid Island, and he fell in love with it and moved his family there. Joseph Silvey died on Reid Island on January 17, 1902; he was sixty-six years old. Only two of Joe and Kwatleemaht's sons returned to Egmont to live. They were Joe Jr. and my grandfather Henry, and they both raised families there. Henry married Amelia Henrietta Andrews. She was Chilean and Squamish; her mother was the daughter of Chief Howe Sound Jim, also known as Chief Squamish Jim. Her father was a Chilean of high-birth who arrived here from Chile in the 1860s. His birth-name was Fidel Sansueza, but the church changed it to Emmanuel Andrews because it was easier for them to pronounce. Henry and Amelia had six children who lived. The eldest was Violet Amelia, the second was my father, Andrew Simmons, though everyone called him Bill, the third was Norman Nookum, the fourth Malcolm Kaiser, the fifth Stanley Telford, and the sixth Juanita Rose.

Sechelt Inlet

Just as we have a notable waterfall in Hotham Sound, we also have a world-class tidal rapids called the Skookumchuck at the entrance to Sechelt Inlet. In the Chinook language it means strong waters. There is no more than twenty minutes of slack water between tides, depending on the tidal difference, and because the shoreline is so crooked and the water has to squeeze between the shore on the west side and the island on the east side, the narrows get very dangerous and full of whirlpools. Dad told me he once saw a long log get sucked down into one of the big ones that forms on the ebb tide just below the island. One time he and his partner lost a lot of shingle bolts when the tugboat captain, Frenchy Fontaine, who was towing their boom, misjudged the turn of the tide. He said those bolts started jumping over the boomsticks like fish, so he and his partner had worked a month for nothing. Most of the local people have learned to live with the danger, but the Skookumchuck still claims the odd person who doesn't respect its awesome power. Dad told me of three sisters named Anderson who perished in the narrows. They made a practice of travelling between Egmont and their home inside the narrows in a big rowboat. As far as I know their bodies were never found. Several times a year people come from all over the world to compete in surfing contests on the standing waves that occur when the tidal differences are large enough to reach maximum speeds. It is amazing to watch those little kayaks doing all their spins, cartwheels and tricks as they compete for major prizes. There is a good trail from Egmont to a viewpoint where you can see this marvellous sight.

My dad worked with Wilf Harper from Pender Harbour not very far in on the north side of Narrows Arm, but he only stayed with Harper until the boom was finished. His camp houses were built on the hillside so their fronts were up on posts. One Sunday they were having lunch when a cougar caught Harper's young dog and was intent on eating her. Harper broke a big heavy homemade hoe over the cougar's head, but it didn't even flinch. So my dad got a big rock and came down with that rock from the porch directly over its head, and that made it drop the dog and jump across the creek where it snarled at them and finally ran away. They took the dog into the house, put it on the table, and after gently washing its intestines off and pushing everything back inside, they sewed her belly up with sewing thread dipped in iodine. They kept her in a box by the stove and she soon healed up. She had a litter of pups a year or so later. The cougar tore the seats out of the boat that was nearby, and they thought he may have been after mice so he must have been really hungry.

The Newcombe Brothers' Story

The following information was provided by Minter (Mint) Newcombe's son, Ken, who was my sister Caroline's first husband and the father of my two nephews, Wayne and Kevin. These are either stories told to him by his dad or from his own recollections.

Eugene, Charlie, Tim and Mint Newcombe handlogged together in the Hotham Sound area from the late 1920s to the early 1930s, and they eventually saved enough between them to purchase a steam donkey that had been built in the early 1900s. But the Depression was a tough time for loggers, and after a few years of just getting by, they decided to part company and try logging on their own. Mint told Ken that after everything was divided up, he came out of the partnership with a hundred dollars in his pocket. Charlie and Eugene set up C & E Logging Ltd. and started high lead logging with a wood-fired steam donkey at Middle Point in Salmon Inlet, close to Misery Creek. As they used wood for the fuel to make steam, their overhead was just the regular wear and tear on the equipment and a little grease. When they eventually sold out to John Bosch, they had a skyline machine as well as a cold decker working.

One time in my early teens I had to spend quite a few days in the hospital, and I was placed in the men's ward with three older guys. I guess it was time to lose my innocence, though even at that my young presence probably caused them to go easy on my education. One of those men was Gene Newcombe, one of the brothers of C & E Logging. Gene had one glass eye that he took out every night before bedtime, and when he was drinking in the beer parlour, he would take his glass eye out and tell it to watch his glass of beer while he went to the bathroom. Gene had the world by the tail, or so he thought, until he got very sick. Then his doctor told him it was terminal and he only had a year to live, so he had better get his affairs in order. So in 1947 he and his brother Charlie sold the company to John Bosch, though Charlie continued to work for the new owner. Gene, who had worked hard for his money, set his mind on spending his share of it, which was half of $30,000, a small fortune in those days, before his time was up. He hired a cab with a younger, like-minded driver, and they headed for California where they went on one big party until all the available money was gone. But at the end of the year he was still going strong, so he figured that either the doctor was wrong or his lifestyle had cured him. In any case, he was sure mad that he had to go back to work to make a living for John Bosch and the outfit he had owned a short time before.

After Charlie and Gene logged for John Bosch for a few more years, they both moved to Quadra Island, and Charlie bought property in Quathiaski Cove from his nephew Bud Jones. Both Charlie and Gene are buried on Quadra. Tim

Newcombe spent his whole life handlogging in Jervis Inlet, and my dad was his partner for quite a while. He was a bit of an acrobat and amazingly wiry and supple. He could stand up and do a summersault in the air and come down on the same spot. Sometimes he would grab a door with his two hands, one some ways below the other, and hold his body horizontal for a short time. When he retired to a nice house in Sechelt, he lived only a few blocks from my dad.

MINTER NEWCOMBE

By Caroline (Newcombe) Jepson

When the brothers went their separate ways in the Depression years, Mint Newcombe also managed to acquire a steam donkey and began logging at Misery Bay in Salmon Inlet with his half-brother, Buster Allen, and his nephew, George Miller, as crew. Quite often they would log all day then after supper work on the boom, putting in a sixteen-hour day if a tug was coming for the boom. In 1944 Mint moved his family to Sechelt so the children could attend school, then he sold his logging camp to Stan Wakefield's brother-in-law, Frank Wilkinson. Just before Easter weekend in 1960 Stan Wakefield and five other crew members from Range Logging Ltd. perished on their way home to Sechelt. Their aluminum outboard boat was found the next day, but their bodies were never found.

Mint's exceptional ability as a donkey puncher and boom man kept him steadily employed until he retired at sixty-five. Three more generations of Mint's family chose logging as a career. Ironically, his great-grandson Ken was killed by a runaway log just a few miles from Mint's old camp at Misery Creek in Salmon Inlet.

John Bosch

I first met and worked with John Bosch about the time he was helping Mac MacDonald with his floating house in Princess Louisa. He had retired from logging, but people who needed something done around the water knew that John was the man to get the job done. One of his customers was the man who owned Pearson Island in the mouth of Agamemnon Channel. This man's small track loader had broken down, and John got me to bring my small Cat over there to pull it down and put it on a float to repair it. In the time we spent together waiting for tides, he told me about coming to Canada as a young man at the beginning of the Great Depression. Not only were jobs scarce, but he had trouble with the language as well. He said that one of his early mining jobs was at the Belmont mine at Surf Inlet on Princess Royal Island, one of the areas where the white Kermode bears live. When they put him to work logging mine props there with horses, even the horses couldn't understand him at first, but when I knew him you could scarcely detect any accent. I have asked his grandson Dean to share the following account of John Bosch's life.

John Bosch with a big fir log: a one-log load. COURTESY BRENDA SILVEY

A BIOGRAPHY OF JOHN BOSCH

by Dean Bosch

John Bosch was born on September 23, 1913, in Groningen, Holland. In 1930, at the age of eighteen, he arrived in Canada by sea, landing at Halifax. He rode the rails across Canada and ended up in Chilliwack where he met his future wife, Dorothy, while working as a labourer picking berries. Throughout the early 1930s, he worked his way up the BC coastline, working for a while at the famous Britannia mines in Howe Sound. Eventually he arrived on the Sunshine Coast and was hired by a pile driving company that drove piles at Davis bay, near Sechelt. When war broke out, he was working for Crucil Logging in Sechelt Inlet, and the company wrote a letter to the government asking for John's exemption from service as he was needed in their logging operations toward the war effort.

During the early 1940s John worked hard for various logging companies, earning his "donkey special" ticket, running steam donkeys and becoming a much in-demand high rigger. He worked six days a week in a tough, dangerous industry and was so in demand with other logging outfits that he would high rig for them on Sundays for some extra income. In 1947 he became independent when he bought the Newcombes' outfit and renamed it the John Bosch Logging Co Ltd. He operated first in Sechelt Inlet and later in outer Jervis Inlet. By this time he and Dorothy and their three children, Dan, Sharon and Dohrn, had shared in the adventure of life in camp in a very remote area, but by 1960 John and Dorothy bought waterfront acreage in Egmont. There they set up a sawmill and float-building business and earned a twenty-five-year contract building floats for the parks board and maintaining the park in Princess Louisa Inlet. By then the Egmont area had become a tourist mecca, spurred on largely by the bountiful salmon harvested in the area. To capitalize on the tourist boom, John moved in cabins from a disbanded logging camp in Vancouver Bay and opened the Egmont Marina Resort and the Skookum Chuck Café & General Store where the Back Eddy Pub now sits today. They provided accommodations, camping, live herring bait and fuel on top of keeping their sawmill active. Around the same time, their son Dan bought a fifty-acre property on Agamemnon Bay, where he and his wife, Dianne, started the Jervis View Marina Resort with houses also purchased from Vancouver Bay. During the logging heyday, the Jervis View Marine Resort also ran a log dump and an active booming ground and provided marina services and moorage for some of the major logging and mining companies in the area.

John and Dorothy eventually sold the marina and moved back to the Sechelt area. He was a dedicated Freemason and donated much of his time with the Masons to improving the community. He also stayed involved with Princess Louisa Inlet Ventures and was hired in 1972 to build a beautiful lodge as a rainy day shelter for boaters and children visiting the inlet; it was named the James F. MacDonald Memorial Lodge. John had known "Mac" very well during Mac's years as the original homesteader in the inlet and was responsible for towing Mac's floathouse to "winter over" in the safe waters of Pender Harbour each year. For nearly sixty years John had lived and worked in this beautiful fjord, and during many of those years provided much-needed employment for local people–as his descendants do to this day.

In his later years John enjoyed winter travels south with Dorothy as well as spending time with his young grandchildren. John passed away after a tough battle with cancer on July 1, 1996, at the age of eighty-three.

Beaver (Treat) Creek in Prince of Wales Reach

Just a mile or so below the big Delta Rock gravel pit at Beaver (Treat) Creek is the scene of a deadly accident in which a good friend of mine was killed. Harry Wise lived the first years of his life in Jervis Inlet where his father, Charlie Wise, (Flo Dubois called him Harry in her book) had a floating store at the site of Malibu Lodge at the entrance to Princess Louisa Inlet. I think Charlie and his oldest son were drowned on a trip to Vancouver for supplies for the store, so when Harry, his brother Dick and sister Phyllis were young, they moved with their mother Lottie to a house in St. Vincent Bay as there was a school there. Dad said they often ran around in the winter without shoes, but they didn't seem to feel the cold. It seems that for some reason Lottie was not able to look after her three remaining kids, and they were placed in an orphanage until they were old enough to look after themselves. Lottie married Pete Hanson, and they had another five kids. When I got to know them all many years later, the Wise and Hanson kids seemed to be one big happy family.

When I worked with Harry, I couldn't believe how tough he was. We were stringing the straw line to a cold deck pile across a small frozen lake on the top of Nelson Island. Harry was the hooker so he took the bight of the strawline and started across the five-hundred-foot-wide lake to avoid the tangle of small trees around the edge. All went well to the middle when we noticed the ice was starting to sink down. Harry came back and tied a couple of boards to his feet to spread his weight and started across again. He got about two-thirds of the way, and he fell through into three feet of water. Since he was closer to the far side, he elected to keep going. He would try to get on top, but the ice just kept breaking under him. It must have taken him the best part of an hour to break his way to the other side. Then he walked all the way around the lake to the spar tree where we had a huge fire waiting for him. He was close to hypothermia, but he reminded us that he had on his Stanfields woollen underwear, and the Stanfield motto was "Even when you are cold and wet, you will feel warm and dry." He didn't look warm and dry.

Harry was one of the few people I've ever known who was always just naturally happy, a joy to work with and be around. He had this infectious giggle that soon had people laughing, so he always had visitors at his home and usually wound up with a party there. He loved his beer and quite a lot of his young friends helped to get rid of any surplus, so to cut down on the expenses, he started to make sake (rice wine). That's when we started to call them "Hari kari and his sake sippers." He had a strong, muscular, perfect body and could press a double-flange cat roller over his head, something I could hardly lift. His brother Dick had that same perfect body and could have been a male model or something. I guess it is all in the genes.

But Harry was one tough hombre, always doing some dangerous trick. One time he had gone up the spar tree in the pass line chain and swung the blocks to the other side of the tree. On the way down when he was out clear of the tree, one minute he was sitting in the pass chain and forty feet off the ground, then he just fell backwards in the chain and caught himself by the feet and hung head-down all the way to the ground.

This fearlessness in the presence of danger is what I think cost him his life. The ground in the area I first mentioned is extremely steep, and Harry was moving a cold deck yarding machine down to the next setting. They had a block purchase on the haulback drum to pull it ahead, and a block on the main drum tailholted to a good big stump to snub it down, so it should have been all right. But Nels Hanson, Harry's half-brother, was there and he said it was not coming down smoothly. It was very jerky, as most likely the machine was breaking over into an even steeper angle and doing a little free run, increasing the strain on the tailholt stump strap. At times like that it is customary to tie the friction lever down, then the engineer gets off until the bad place is past. But they didn't do that and the strap finally broke due to the extreme strain. Harry should never have been on that machine, but he was right by the head block on the front of the sleigh when the strap broke. He couldn't escape all the cables that were lashing around and he was killed instantly. The engineer was badly injured and died in hospital in Vancouver without regaining consciousness. The machine was wrecked as it tore down the mountain.

Harry was buried in the cemetery at Whiskey Slough in Pender Harbour where he had made his home. He left a big family of brothers and sisters, many close friends and his grieving widow, Celina. Harry was such a big, good-natured guy that the funeral had to be held in the community hall, which was right full. Harry's friends fought tears as they paid their respects that day, and in the middle of the service Canon Alan Greene had to pause for a moment to compose himself, as he had married Harry and Celina only a few years before.

My good friend Harry Wise and Joan Russell. Harry's giggle was contagious.
COURTESY THE SWAN FAMILY

Logging at Beaver (Treat) Creek

Old Bob Campbell was a colourful storyteller. My dad said old Bob told him that he was out hunting one time when he fell down hard and put a bend in his gun barrel, but he picked himself up and continued hunting. He jumped a big buck that took off and ran around a bluff, but Bob fired anyway, and the bullet from that bent barrel went right around the bluff and killed the deer. But tall tales don't put logs in the water, and Old Bob got into financial difficulties. He had a camp and a steam donkey as well as some fine timber on a very steep sidehill at Beaver (Treat) Creek near the present Delta Rock gravel operation. Fortunately, my uncles Pete and John Klein had a nearly new D8 Cat but no timber, so they teamed up with Campbell, but they had a few mishaps before all the kinks were ironed out of their operation. Their camp was across the Beaver Creek canyon from the logging operation, so the first thing they had to do was move the camp. They rigged up a skyline and began moving the buildings safely across, one by one. The last one was the cookhouse, the biggest building in the camp. They decided to leave all the dishes and small things inside

Pete and John Klein once tried to move a cookhouse across Treat Creek. It never made it. COURTESY JOHN KLEIN

and brace it all up for strength, then away it went. Everything was going just fine when, right in the middle of the canyon, something let go and the cookhouse was no more.

After the camp was finished, they began work on the chute and the road. The chute, which was two thousand feet long, worked too well as the logs hit the chuck too fast, and many that went down butt first would split in half when they hit the water. They were able to beat this problem by sending down double-length logs, top end first, and the boom men cut them in two with a dragsaw when they were in the water. My dad was their boom man at that time, and when the logs began to pour in, he was fairly busy. I was about five years old, and I can remember the big splashes when those logs hit the chuck. (I also remember the Union boat going by, and the water was so calm that I thought there were big fish following the boat. Later, I found out it was just the boat's wake.)

They decided to use the Cat to access the timber that was farther up the mountainside. They would use the steam donkey to yard the logs to a spar tree and the Cat to swing the logs down a road where they could push them into the chute that took them into the saltchuck. But before they really got going, Uncle John Cline lost the Cat in the chute. He had just brought a load of logs down, and he stopped the Cat to remove a rock so the machine wouldn't have to bounce over it. Instead of setting the foot brakes, he just pulled the drum brake on, expecting the turn of logs to hold the machine on the steep grade. But the brake handle on that Cat took about ninety pounds to snap it over centre, so I would guess that in his haste to get the rock out of his way, he didn't get it fully engaged. As his feet hit the track, the brake let go, and as the top track moves at twice the speed of the machine, it shot him out ahead of the Cat where luckily he landed on his feet running. There was a brow log that forced him to run for his life until he could duck behind the log as the machine unwound the mainline and went thundering past him and down the chute. At the first turn it jumped the chute and got stopped by a stump. They had to bring the big steam donkey down from the woods to pull the Cat back from where it landed, a slow miserable job.

There were some houses there for married men, so Dad got one and moved the whole family up Jervis for the summer. The camp tender wasn't big enough for all of us, so we rode with a guy named Frank "Frenchy" Fontaine, who had a forty-foot boat that he ran up and down the inlet with passengers and freight on a regular basis. It was called the *Dangler*. Fontaine had a thick French-Canadian accent, and to welcome his passengers onboard, he gave a little speech in his best King

Many people settled in Queens Reach, Jervis Inlet. Frenchy Fontaine, who is holding the knife, showed up at this picnic, and so did Charlie Whittaker, who's at the extreme right. COURTESY LINDA MATTIS

Frank Fontaine used the Dangler *for hauling freight, passengers and sometimes towing.* COURTESY LINDA MATTIS

James English. It went something like this: "Welcome to de *Dang-ler*, (heavy on the last syllable). Our trip will take some time, so make yourselfs comfortable, and lad-ees, if you 'ave to hevacuate, you can go into de little room in de back of de boat and shit in da bucket." I remember the boat but don't recall much about the man, though Dad said he was very good-natured.

For most of our time in that camp I had two girls for playmates, Mickey and Irene Harper, one older and the other younger than me, and for a couple of months we played on the beach in front of the houses. Then after one fateful day, they were not allowed to play with me anymore. When kids are having fun, there is a tendency to put off going to the bathroom until things are desperate. It seems that I had neglected to go up to the outhouse until it was too late, so I took my pants down and started to pee. I guess the girls had no brothers and didn't know boys had different equipment, so they came right over to see this great phenomenon. Now, being the centre of attention, I put on maximum pressure and shot a stream higher than my head. When the show was over, I pulled up my pants, and we went on playing. When the girls told their mother, they were never allowed to play with that dirty little Phillips boy again. But I was going to be six that December and was needed to make up the eight students necessary to get a teacher for the Kleindale School anyway, so in September we moved back to Pender Harbour.

Vancouver Bay

At 11 p.m. on Sunday, June 17, 1792, Captain George Vancouver anchored his two small survey boats in the bay that was eventually given his name. It is a good size and provides safe shelter in most winds, but according to Vancouver's log, it was pouring rain and they all chose to sleep by a fire on the beach. He had every hope that Jervis Inlet, or as he called it Jervis's Canal, was the much-looked-for Northwest Passage. The next day he came to the end of it and began the long journey back to Nelson Island. More than a hundred years later when old Charles Roscoe Johnstone moved his large family from Earls Cove into Vancouver Bay, they became the first white people to live in the Bay. And this is where Ivan Johnstone, the first white baby born in this place, arrived in 1905.

In the late 1920s David Jeremiason, who'd had an interest in Booth Logging before it was burned out at Freil Lake in 1919, brought together some people with sufficient capital to start a big railroad show in Vancouver Bay. He used the same locomotive from his last show. My dad said it took a year or more plus $250,000 before they put the first log in the water. Dad ran the supply boat at first and then was assigned to a construction crew. His boss was Olaus Lee, the brother of Ole Lee who was the father of the big Lee family of Pender Harbour. Dad had never seen what could be done by someone who could really use a carpenter's square, and he told me how Olaus Lee took the square and marked all the posts the big oil tank platform was to be built on. It was about twenty-five feet across and needed about a dozen posts set on a sloping rocky beach. But when the posts were cut on his marks with all their different angles, they all fit perfectly. Then he marked out a pattern for a rim around the tank on top of the decking, and the last piece just dropped into place. He was a master builder disguised as a dumb fisherman. Olaus Lee had the property in Agamemnon Bay, which is now called Moccasin Valley, where he built and repaired fishboats. (His son, Robert Olaus Lee, was my partner in Phillips and Lee Logging Co.) David Jeremiason—everyone just called him Jerry—hired a lot of local men for the construction as well as the logging operation later, and all the men I knew who ever worked for him said

This picture came with the caption "Logging in Vancouver Bay." There's no one alive who can confirm exactly what it's showing. COURTESY BRENDA SILVEY

what a great boss he was. Dad introduced me to him at Wilf Klein's funeral because Wilf had worked for him when he was a teenager with his dad, Fred, almost fifteen years before. Jeremiason had come up from Vancouver to pay his respects.

The last big operator in Vancouver Bay was BC Forest Products. They had a big truck operation, and after they were through and moved the camp out, they built a really nice lodge where officials of this large BC-wide company and their guests would go to hunt and fish. For a few years I was a salmon enhancement board member, representing commercial fishermen, and one of my fellow board members was Gerry Burch, a senior vice-president of BC Forest Products, representing the forest industry. At the time we were trying to transplant pink salmon into the Vancouver River from the Skwakwa River and had a small hatchery there. One day they took some of the board members there on a tour by water taxi and the lodge supplied our meal, compliments of Mr. Burch. I haven't heard how the transplant is doing now, but at the time, in spite of a lot of problems with flooding of the facilities, it seemed to be a success. The company has since given the lodge to the Sechelt Native Band.

Lord Fisher

My dad always had a boat of some kind, so if he needed a job, he would just go around to the camps and ask if they needed a man. He preferred the job of boom man, but being both a logger and a fisherman, he was a good all-round man, and having worked around Jervis Inlet for so many years, he had built up a good reputation. Once, when he had been unable to find a job at any of the camps where he had worked in past years, he wound up working for a guy that the locals called "Lord Fisher" because of his dignified British ways. Dad, who came from the lower working class, found this distasteful. Fisher was working at the mouth of High Creek on the north shore of Vancouver Bay. Fisher's wife was a Chinese woman he had married when he worked in China years before, and they had two sons who helped their dad, mostly handlogging. But this time they were logging with a donkey and needed more men, so dad worked with them for a few months until he could find work more to his liking. Mostly in later years he worked as boom foreman for Jim Peterson and Frank Kuchinka, who had a big outfit in St. Vincent Bay.

Stakawus and Glacier Creeks

In 1934 after the Gustavson Brothers, Eric and Thure, had finished logging all the timber at Misery Creek in Salmon Inlet, they moved their big railroad logging camp to Stakawus or Slate Creek on the east side of Princess Royal Reach. It was named for the big deposit of slate, and at one time there was a quarry operating here. A little further down that reach is Glacier Creek where a big camp operated for many years. Among the last loggers to work there were the Dougan brothers who came after they were finished at Anderson Bay at the south end of Texada Island. Charles, Dave and Garth Dougan logged there for a few years and then finally moved up to Jackson Bay by Wellbore Rapids. After he retired, Charles wrote a book called *My Daughter's Request: Spotlight on the Yesterday of Country Folk* (Alexco Enterprises, Duncan, BC, 1991), which is a history of the Dougan family's logging struggles from their beginnings at Shawnigan Lake.

Just below Glacier Creek at the end of the straight beach where the shoreline takes a bulge around Moorsam Bluffs is a place that Basil Joe said his elders called Kohts-lah'-ko, which translates as "the place where a man cannot drown." There is a fairly large creek tumbling down the hillside here, and it enters the saltwater with great force through a small split in the rocks. The fresh water is all frothed up with air as it falls over the bluff, and it grabs more air just as it hits the water. As a result of all this air being driven so deep down, all these bubbles keep coming up and the whole area is covered with foam. They say the bubbles of air that get trapped under your body will prevent you from sinking. If you're following the beach going south on that side of the inlet, you can see the foam from quite a distance.

Moorsam Bluffs is where Basil Joe claims his ancestors would send young men up to where the mountain goats were feeding on the bluffs. Then they made a lot of noise and chased the goats over the bluffs, where they were picked up by others in canoes. This was one of the few ways they could catch one. Another place that was important to the First Nations culture was on the west side of the inlet between Osgood Creek and Patrick Point where there's a steeply sloping smooth area about two hundred feet long that looks black from a distance. They called it Yay-klay'-nahss or Running Slippery Rock, and it was a place of testing for young men for the entrance into manhood. The test was to run full speed across a certain portion of it in bare feet without falling or slipping into the chuck. The next test was to dive off a fifty-foot-high piece of granite called Kwuh-oh'-tah that had separated from the bluff a short ways up toward Patrick Point. If they could do these two things, they were really men.

The Brittain River Fire

In August 1951 a huge forest fire started up by Brittain River on the west side of Prince of Wales Reach and burned down to Hotham Sound and over the mountain toward Lois Lake before it was put out. In those days the Forest Service had emergency powers that allowed the forest ranger to conscript any able-bodied man to go and fight fire. My old partner was one of the ones who had to go. But one guy resented the press gang method so much that he was wearing his spiked caulk boots and walked on the nice varnished decks of the forestry boat before they could stop him. He said to my partner, "Listen to them caulks bite in!"

But there was not much the Forest Service could do about this fire except watch it burn. In Hotham Sound it burned from the beach to the top of the mountains, and it was such a hot fire that it burned the soil right up, so when it went out, there was only ash on top of bare rock. Sixty-five years have passed and there is still a lot of rock showing. It burned through the low pass between Lena Lake and McMurray Bay, from up by Brittain River. At Oscar Neimi's workings they managed to save the camp buildings but lost most everything else. Later Ollie Sladey moved many of the buildings to

Pender Harbour, and the big cookhouse became the Legion hall in Pender Habour. It was moved in two pieces by Dubois Logging for free and reconstructed by mostly volunteer labour. Over the years different operations have worked at salvaging the burnt cedar in Brittain River for shakes. There is about twelve miles of logging road up the left side of the Brittain River, and there was a bridge across it, which was burned, but the scars from that 1951 fire are healing, and some day Brittain River will be logged again. In the 1980s there was a prison camp there and inmates could participate in special programs to be better able to rejoin society after they were released.

Oliver Larson at Osgood Creek

In 1967 Bob O. Lee and I went for a deal in Vanguard Bay, but we needed a welder and heard about one for sale at Osgood Creek, which is between Brittain River and Patrick Point, where a guy named Oliver Larson had been operating for years. He was a big, good-looking, tough logger about forty-five years old and had come down from Palmer Bay in Discovery Passage to start one of the tougher shows in Jervis Inlet. I was chosen to go up there in our little fifteen-foot runabout to check out the welder. When I got there, everyone except old Charlie, the cook, was up in the woods so I had to wait till five o'clock when they came in. I decided the welder was a good deal, but my little boat was too small so we agreed on a price and I would come up later with my gillnet boat to get the machine. By this time the sea was very rough because that part of Princess Royal Reach is the worst stretch for winds. When the sun shines in the interior of the province, the air that is heated starts to rise, and to replace it, the cool air from the coast is sucked up through all the coastal inlets. From noon to almost dark, the winds can really get going, so I stayed the night at Osgood Creek and left next morning when it was flat calm. My partner, who should have known better, was sure sore at me as he was worried that something had happened to me. He said, "You should have come anyway. It never gets that rough in Jervis Inlet."

The next week we went up there in a thirty-four-foot boat to get the welder. Oliver was there, and Bob loved to talk. On top of this, old Charlie was running off a batch of what they called "white lightning." It was double distilled then run through a big cotton-filled funnel and a bowl full of charcoal so it was crystal clear and just like gasoline for power. We had to wait until it cooled so we could pass judgment on it, though one sip was enough for me. By the time we got the welder aboard, there were six-foot swells rolling by out in the inlet. So remembering what Bob had said about it never blowing in Jervis Inlet, I said, "Come on, Bob. It's time to go." He thought maybe we should stay the night. I reminded him that "it never blows in Jervis." We waited till next morning.

Larson built a big house on the waterfront at Egmont, and he went there every winter when he couldn't log in Osgood due to the snow. At the time we had a winter show on Nelson Island and ended up hiring his Wagner Skidder to swing our logs when the haul got too long for our Cat. One day we were visiting the Larsons in their new house at Egmont, and we were all having tea when there was a sort of a muffled explosion. The Department of Highways was blasting rock up on the side of the road, so we assumed that was what it was. A few minutes later it happened again, but it seemed to come from the area of Oliver's big liquor bar. As they looked a bit closer, a lot of liquid was coming out on the floor from under the bar. It turned out that Oliver had brought several gallon jugs of his "white lightning" down from camp, and as the temperature in the new house built up, so did the pressure in the jugs. He quickly loosened the tops before the rest exploded, too. He didn't seem to worry that the law might catch him.

Another story about Oliver's still that made the rounds went like this. There was a rumour that the police were going to be checking around looking for it, so he and his crew dismantled it, and some of the boys took it up the logging road to hide it until the crisis was over. But when they went to get it, they had hidden it so well that it couldn't be found.

I don't want to give the impression that Oliver was a drunk, far from it. He was all business whenever I was around him. When we hunted together up on Potato Mountain at Tatlayoko Lake in the Chilcotin, Oliver and I were at the upper reaches of the mountain, it was getting late and we were bringing down two big bucks when we looked across a deep ravine and about 150 yards away there was a huge three-point standing there broadside. I was against shooting it as it would be dark before we could flounder across the ravine, gut it and move it. But Oliver wanted that deer, so we both got ready and fired together, and down that deer went. So we left our two bucks with a piece of clothing with man smell on it to keep the wolves away and made our way over

Oliver and Ruby Larson lived in a house on the waterfront in Egmont.
COURTESY BRENDA SILVEY

to the other side, tended to this deer then left him like the other two. It was nearly midnight before we stumbled into camp, and the other six guys in the party were about to send a search party up to find us. Some of them came up with us the next day to drag our meat out.

Oliver didn't know the meaning of quit, and that's the way he faced life. When things got easier, he moved his wife, Ruby, and kids into that fine new house on the waterfront in Egmont. Both he and Ruby have passed away, leaving a large family to carry on, some in the logging industry.

Deserted Bay (Tsonei)

For centuries before Europeans came, the First Nations people had a large village called Tsonei at the mouth of the Deserted River, which is right across Queens Reach from Patrick Point. The river valley goes back for miles following the river, and the best chum salmon run in the inlet goes up it to spawn in the fall. This place was very important to the Native people because of the clam beds there as well.

Part of Gustavson's camp at Deserted Bay. COURTESY BEA SWANSON

After the Gustavsons finished railroad logging at Stakawus Creek, they moved their camp to the north side of Deserted River, where they switched to truck logging. This was one of the most productive camps in the inlet from 1938 to 1951 when the Gustavsons sold it to North Shore Timber Co. The brothers retired, but Eric's son, Arnold, stayed on until all the timber was logged. The good news is that after the passing of all these years the logging scars there have healed, and the fish habitat is good enough to have supported a historic-sized run of chum salmon a few years back.

Eric Gustavson and his foreman, another Swedish man named Adolph Swanson, had married two sisters, and after World War II Swanson's son, Harold, married Bea Spanks and they moved up to Deserted Bay in 1946 or '47 and worked there until 1953. It wasn't new territory for Bea as she had lived at Bloomberg's camp with her dad and mom as a small girl. Bea was still living in her own apartment in Sechelt in her nineties when she gave me most of the pictures and stories of the Gustavsons' camp that I've used in this book. She also wrote the following memories of her time as a small girl when she was at Bloomberg's.

Harold and Bea Swanson married after World War II. They worked in Deserted Bay until 1953. COURTESY BEA SWANSON

BLOOMBERG'S CAMP IN JERVIS INLET

by Bea Swanson

Bloomberg's camp was in Jervis Inlet about three miles north of Brittain River. It only operated for two or three years before going bankrupt because of the Depression and a series of bad luck. The owner was Andy Bloomberg. He and his wife, Anna, had two children–Elvin, who later became known as Andy and moved to Merritt, and Evelyn, who married Lloyd Gale. My father, Harry Spanks, went to camp as the cook, and my mother, Edna, and their four children, Merle, Bea, Anna and Vic, were the only family in camp. My mother home schooled her three oldest children as she had been a teacher previously in Nova Scotia.

The camp had a wooden chute running from the woods to the saltchuck. Logs would sometimes jump out of the chute and land in the creek alongside and kick up rocks, which landed on the buildings close by. One rock landed on the bed where my mother had been sitting a minute before. She was called to come and see the logs hitting the creek and had taken a couple of steps from where she had been sitting, otherwise she could have been killed. The cookhouse, bunkhouses, and the accommodations for our family were moved the next day. Some of the crew were Ira Vicson, cousin Bert, and a Mr. Emrick–these are all I can remember. They were all Swede Finns and had all left families in Sweden. They didn't collect their wages, so when Andy Bloomberg went bankrupt, they were also left with nothing. Bert was killed when a limb fell on his head–there were no hard hats in those days or for years after.

The men spoiled us kids, building sleds for us in the winter. They also built a flat-bottomed boat, so on July 1 the whole camp decided to go on a picnic in this boat and a rowboat, thirteen of us in all. Andy's family had come up for the summer, and Norman and Ben Klein from Pender Harbour had come as well. Mrs. Bloomberg had a fit as she thought thirteen people was too much of a load. Anyway, we got to Brittain River, and four of us kids got out of the boat and ran up the bank to a big huckleberry bush. I slipped and fell against a small tree stump that had been cut off at an angle, and it took a piece out of my leg. It didn't cut any arteries or cords, so even though it was very deep, it didn't bleed much. We broke into Mr. [Teddy] Groven's prospecting cabin to try and find something to put on the cut, but there was only iodine, and they wouldn't use that. We had to go back to the camp, and as it always blows during the afternoon, we had a slow, rough ride. Then I had to sit in camp from Sunday to Tuesday before the boat came. I think it was the *Comox*. At Sechelt we had to stay at Bert Whitaker's second hotel and caught the boat to Vancouver the next day. I couldn't walk until September, and by then we had ended up in West Vancouver. My dad had to quit his job and collect his wages, but we heard the rest of the crew weren't so lucky. A guy named Huber from Pender Harbour took over the cook's job from my dad.

At the time of Bea's accident there was no hospital on the east side of Georgia Strait between Powell River and Vancouver. The Columbia Coast Mission hospital in Pender Harbour opened two years after her accident. Bea finished her schooling in Vancouver, but after she married Harold Swanson, they moved up to the Gustavsons' camp in Deserted Bay where they lived in a shake house that Harold's father, Adolph or "Swannie," had paid fifty dollars for. Harold added a bathroom and two bedrooms on a log sleigh and when they left in 1953, they set off to tow the addition down to Porpoise Bay. But the barge it was on broke loose in the middle of the Skookumchuck Narrows, and the house rode through by itself. They moved it onto a lot in Sechelt and built some more rooms on to it, and it is still standing proudly for all to see with its new kitchen and living room at 5773 Mermaid Street in Sechelt.

While they lived in Deserted Bay, Bea and Harold had three kids, so Bea was kept very busy as a young mother in what was a beautiful wilderness area, which she came to love very much. As they were without refrigeration, they canned a lot of venison and fish. A school was started for the kids of the many married loggers, and a young man named Arno Ulmer came to teach. After he moved to Pender Harbour,

Moving a steam donkey on the last logging railroad on the mainland at Stakawus, or Slate Creek, just a few miles south of Deserted Bay. COURTESY BEA SWANSON

This spar tree was 140 feet long. COURTESY BEA SWANSON

Three steam donkeys use the 140-foot spar tree. One is loading logs, one is yarding around the spar tree and one is hooked to a skyline. This is a rare and unusual picture of steam donkey logging. The process used more rigging than a sailing schooner. COURTESY BEA SWANSON

Truck logging replaced railroad logging at Deserted Bay. COURTESY BEA SWANSON

Earl Hilsden was the teacher for both the loggers' kids and the Native children who lived across the bay.

Harold Swanson was one of those MacGyver-type of guys who could do most anything from running his own trapline to constructing beautiful clinker-built rowboats. When the camp at Deserted Bay was closed, he was responsible for moving the buildings to Lew Milligan's new operation at Vanguard Bay. After Harold and Bea moved to Sechelt, Harold and his brother started Swanson's Ready-Mix, and over the years Bea had a major part in the growth of this successful company. Harold passed away a few years ago after many happy years of retirement, and Bea died in February 2014.

A Wilderness Family

No book about Jervis Inlet would be complete without the story of the Johnstones, who were among the first few white people to move into the area. The father, Charles Roscoe Johnstone, was a mountain man from Kentucky who met his wife, Dora, in a small Colorado town where she was teaching school. They married after a whirlwind courtship and promptly left on horseback for the wandering life of a gold miner. Their oldest son, Forrest or Judd, was born in Kansas in 1891, and more children were born as they moved from one placer claim to another. Then Charles heard the nuggets were bigger and easier to find in Canada and Alaska, so the whole family hit the trail by horses and covered wagon for the Pacific coast. Most of this family history was passed down by Judd, a quiet-talking man but a great storyteller, and no one spent much time in the area without hearing about the amazing things his father did in those early years. Many times I heard about Charles Roscoe Johnstone outrunning a fast horse in a hundred-yard dash and being able to fire his single-shot rifle as fast as a lever action by putting cartridges between the fingers of his left hand ahead of time. He lived off the land, hunting, fishing, handlogging and trapping, and he trained all his children to do the same. The girls could shoot game along with the best of them, and one of the boys is said to have shot a cougar at eight years old.

The family stuck together and worked their way up Jervis to pursue fresh trapping, hunting and handlogging areas. When they landed in Deserted Bay, there was a good-sized First Nations village, Tsonei or Ts'unay there, but they interacted well with their Native neighbours and were still there when two more children were born, Bruce (1909) and Katherine (1913), with Charles acting as the midwife. What a pioneer woman Dora must have been, living in a cramped house made out of shakes with no proper stove to cook on, often getting her own wood and water, and home schooling her big family. In spite of all the hardships, she never seems to have seen it as a great hardship, following her man all over the continent and providing for her loved ones as she did. Next, the Johnstones moved inside the rapids at Princess Louisa Inlet, living in another hand-split cedar shake house on the only flat ground there.

The story going around was that after World War I, when a big logging camp moved into Deserted Bay, the Johnstones thought it was getting too crowded and got in their boats and headed for Alaska. Steve and another one of the brothers, Ivan, the first Johnstone born in this area, stayed behind in Princess Louisa to look after the place, but Ivan died in the great flu epidemic in 1919 and is said to be buried at Malibu. Judd and Frank had signed up in the US Army at the beginning of the war, but Frank was killed in action, so when Judd came back, he went with the family to Alaska. Kathrene Pinkerton in her book *Three's a Crew* (Carrick and Evans, 1940, and Horsdal & Schubart, 1991) mentions the Johnstones and describes them as being a well-rounded, happy family, living in four new shake houses in the Behm Canal, not too far from Ketchikan, where they were making a good living from handlogging and trapping. Even old Charles would enjoy a movie when the family spent some time in the winter in Ketchikan.

Judd was in love with Dora Ellen Jeffries, a girl who had lived in Princess Louisa when her father, Bob Jefferies, lived there, and one winter Judd ran his boat all the way from Alaska and took his new bride back with him. But she didn't like Alaska, and to please her he came back to Jervis Inlet after a few years. Their children were Thelma, Grace, Evelyn, Alice, Frank, Bob and Chris. The first two were born in Alaska where the family lived out in the wilds in a tent. Back in Princess Louisa, they had very few visitors, and any supplies or business required a rowboat trip to Pender Harbour, an eighty-plus-knot round trip. The beautiful high mountains on the south side make it a dreary place in the winter, and for days at a time the clouds are so low that you can't see more than a few hundred feet up the mountains. Sometimes in the coldest part of winter when the whole inlet froze over, Judd and Dora and their family would be locked in, so they moved to Nelson Island in the early 1930s, and Judd found work on nearby Hardy Island. After a few years living in the quarry house, Judd built a big two-storey house where they were pretty comfortable, considering where they lived before. I saw the Johnstone house for the first time as a twelve-year-old when my dad and I made a fishing trip to Blind Bay. It sat on a rocky knoll with a full view of Blind Bay all around.

I didn't meet Judd until 1946, and by that time his hair was white. He was a tall, good-looking man, very soft-spoken and courteous, a real gentleman. Shortly after this he bought my

Uncle Pete's gillnet boat, the *Anda*, when Pete started logging with my dad in Cockburn Bay. It would seem that some of Judd's brothers and sisters as well as his parents may have stayed in Alaska, and some could still be there. Dora, Judd's wife and constant companion, died in 1965 after more than twenty-five years at Blind Bay. Judd died four years later. His old Blind Bay neighbours missed his cheery smile and timely stories.

Judd's sons Frank and Chris became well-known loggers and tree fallers. Like his dad, Frank was a big, friendly bear of a man with a reputation for being able to hold a small direct-drive chainsaw in one hand and plunge-cut the bar right through a log. Most guys can't do that with two hands. I got to know him in the 1980s when he decided to turn his last boat, the *Larry H*, into a gillnetter. Henry Harris and his wife, Sis, took him under their wing and brought him up to speed on what was needed. In the mid-1980s I bought a big boat and began cash-buying salmon in the areas that Frank chose to fish, and if he was around, he always sold me his fish. Last May when I talked to him on the phone, he was in his nineties, living in Powell River, and even though he said he had health challenges, he sounded bright as a penny.

Some of the Johnstone girls married local men. Grace married Dick Krentz, Evelyn married Johnny Vaughn (who died after inhaling exhaust fumes in his gasboat), and Thelma, after losing her first husband, married Slim Deberri.

One of my best friends and hunting buddies was Richard—or as he was better known, "Parky"—Higgins, and he told me that his dad, Charlie, knew the Johnstones well. Charlie was originally from Lasqueti Island where Higgins Island was named after the family. The island is very close to the beach on the west shore of False Bay on the southwest side

Hugh Henry (Harry) Higgins was a veteran of the British forces, and his son, Charlie, was one of the best rifle shots I have ever seen. COURTESY MARIE REID

of Lasqueti. Charlie's father, Hugh Henry (Harry) Higgins, was a veteran of the British forces that kept the peace in BC, and when he was discharged in 1882, he filed for a crown grant to pre-empt land on Lasqueti. He married a young half-Native girl named Mary Ann Jefferies, and as a sort of a dowry he is said to have given two sacks of flour, a canoe and other things to her family, the Jefferies of Maple Bay on Lasqueti. Harry and Mary Ann had two kids, Charles and Mary. Then over the years the Higginses became close friends with Bill Rouse and his wife, Margret, from Rouse's Bay on the other end of the island, and I guess one day they got too close and decided to make a wife swap. Charlie's mother went with Rouse who in 1909 took his family to live at Earls Cove then to the Pender Harbour area. Charlie stayed with his dad and Margret until he was on his own as a teenager and became acquainted with the Johnstone boys and moved in with them in Jervis Inlet. Charlie Higgins—or as Parky called him, "Pappy"—told Parky all the same stories that Judd Johnstone told, including the one about Charles Johnstone Sr., when he needed money for a trip to the coast, going into a saloon and, after talking it up for a while, taking bets that he could beat their fastest horse in a hundred-yard dash. He was well over six feet tall and long-legged and could really run. They didn't know that it takes a while for a horse to reach its speed, but a man takes only a few feet, so he always won the money.

Charlie Higgins also confirmed Judd's stories about the Johnstone boys going out with a rifle, a little ammunition, some salt and a few matches and living by their wits for a week to prove to their father that they were ready to be called "Mountain Men." Later they added a new wrinkle: they couldn't share their meat with each other, and that would have sharpened their hunting skills. Charlie Higgins joined the fun and sometimes won these Mountain Man contests. The Johnstone boys and Charlie Higgins would race to the top of Hunaechin Mountain, the tall, cone-shaped mountain at the head of Jervis Inlet, and when the first Johnstone boy

Old Harry Higgins' two children, Charlie and Mary. Note that Charlie's not wearing glasses. For years he used a rifle with a broken sight, and at the age of eighty-five was still winning shooting contests.
COURTESY MARY ANN JEFFRIES

broke over the top, there was Charlie waiting for him. Basil Joe said that, being raised next door to the Johnstone family in Deserted Bay, he often went on their "wildman hunts," too, and also raced them up Hunaechin Mountain.

Charlie Higgins said that, except when it was a contest or something else he enjoyed doing, Steve Johnstone was pretty lazy and hard to get up in the morning. Right by his bed he had a knothole that he would use on a regular basis to relieve himself so he wouldn't have to get up. One morning the rest of the boys were waiting for it when it came out through the knothole, and without making a sound they gently clamped on an old fish head with all those sharp teeth in its mouth. They could hear Steve pleading, "Nice kitty-kitty, nice kitty!" Then someone had to laugh and "let the cat out of the bag."

Charlie said that another time Steve was standing up and relieving himself over the side of a small gasboat as they were travelling across the bay. He was standing right alongside the engine, and someone—without thinking that he would take him up on it—dared him to be brave enough to put it on the sparkplug. Steve had most likely never had any experience with engines and certainly had never been bit by a spark-plug shock. When the spark travelled up that tender member, Steve's legs straightened out so fast that he just shot up and over the side, so they had to do a man-overboard rescue. This was a classic Steve Johnstone story, one that was told whenever men were discussing him, so I think it is true.

In his younger days Steve was briefly married to one of the Jefferies girls, Clara, and they had one daughter, Caroline, but the marriage didn't last as he yearned for the wilds of Jervis Inlet and spent the rest of his life up by Malibu. He would work for Gustavson or Oscar Neimi, cutting wood or acting as "whistlepunk" or hiring out as camp watchman to make just enough to get by on, along with his trapping. Steve was used to roughing it and was often seen barefoot, even in the winter. Being raised with the Native village close by, he had trained himself like the Native boys to ignore cold and pain by taking a morning swim, and so he got the reputation of being just as tough as the Native boys. One time when my partner Bob Lee was working for Oscar Neimi at Brittain River, Steve had been working there for some months and decided to take a time-out, so he just took to the mountains that he loved and went camping. While he was gone, they found where he'd been living up beyond the tailblocks of the highest cold decker in a cave with a fire out front and a pile of cans, which was enough, along with the game he knew how to trap, to last him a couple of weeks.

One day in 1960 my partner and I were working right next to the Garden Bay pub, so we were having a beer before going home for the day when this old guy with a big white beard came through the door and introduced himself as Steve Johnstone from Princess Louisa Inlet. He was all dressed up in a new shirt and denim pants. After an unbroken fourteen-year spell in the inlet he was out on the town and seemed like he was looking for a good time. He looked just like Gabby Hayes, the movie actor, and he kept laughing, "Hee-hee-hee." Some other sources say that, in fact, he took an annual trip to Vancouver, often coming back with his nails painted and lipstick here and there. Steve was struck and killed by a car on the street in Vancouver in the late 1960s.

My friend Parky Higgins told me a few funny things that happened to him over the years. He called himself "Joe Btfsplk," after the sad little man in Al Capp's comic strip

My friend Richard (Parky) Higgins had the worst luck in the world but could always laugh about it. COURTESY BRENDA SILVEY

Li'l Abner. The sun could be shining all over, but a little black cloud always followed Joe around, just raining on him alone. But most of Parky's bad fortune was of his own making and his inattention to details. When he was first married, he bought the old Pender Harbour school ferry *Romany Chal* (*Gypsy Girl*) from Les Wilkinson when Les went to the bigger *Dakota Belle.* Parky had the back cabin removed and converted it to a thirty-six-foot double-ended troller, which he used to fish in the summer. When he finished fishing for the year, he went up to L M and N Logging, just inside the Sechelt Narrows, tied up to their big log float and walked up to the camp to try for a job. He didn't know that the boom man was getting ready to dynamite the big float to kill the toredos or shipworms that bore into the floats. While Parky was gone, the boom man set off a series of small, evenly spaced charges, and when Parky came back, his boat was hanging on the lines, sunk. He had to tie logs alongside it to take it down to his father-in-law, Bill Silvey, to have it recaulked. There was a big mess of oil from the bilge and other water damage to clean up, and he had no insurance and no winter job either.

A few years later Parky and his brother-in-law Gene Silvey

were on a hunting trip inside Sechelt Inlet. They had hunted the north shore of Salmon Arm, which ends at Clowhom Falls, which used to be the main source of power for the Sechelt Peninsula, and started following along the beach on the south shore. It was high tide and raining, so they had the door closed and were both standing in the cabin with two loaded rifles. All of a sudden there was a huge bang and they thought that the rifles had gone off as they were nearly deafened by the noise. What had happened was that the boat's thirty-foot left trolling pole, which had a metal stay-wire, had struck the high voltage power line that was strung across the bay, and the juice found its way to ground in the saltwater by jumping from the stay-wire to the steering chain and rudder. When they got brave enough to look around, they found all the links of the steering chain were welded together. If either of them had been standing with their hands on the wheel, they would have been most likely killed. There had been warning signs that they failed to see, but Parky could always laugh at his misfortune. He was a pleasure to be around.

Parky's dad, Charlie Higgins, was one of the best rifle shots I have ever seen, and he kept his family fed for years with his 30-30 rifle. Parky told me that his dad broke the front sight on that rifle and went on using it that way for years. When asked how he did it, he said, "You can point your finger, can't you?" One day at a turkey shoot we had twenty guys lined up for a hundred-yard offhand rifle shoot. Only six guys were able to hit the six-inch bull. Old Charlie, at eighty-five years of age and using his seal gun, a 222, plunked it right in the middle. But he used to make his living on seal bounties, so we didn't have a chance.

Princess Louisa Inlet

It has been said by people who have travelled the world and viewed all its beauty spots that two places stand out as the greatest mountain scenery in the world. One is Princess Louisa and the other is Milford Sound in New Zealand. I have seen both, and they are very beautiful, but quite different. The mountains around Milford Sound are not as high as Princess Louisa and are covered with pretty foliage, which is spectacular, but to see it at its best, you have to come after a heavy rain, just as the clouds over the mountains are clearing, because within half an hour all the hundreds of waterfalls start to dry up. There are boats with the capacity to take four hundred people at a time for cruises out to the ocean entrance seven miles away, and they repeat this all day as the people arrive by land buses.

Princess Louisa is about twenty-five miles from Egmont, the nearest town, and while there are tours available, I doubt we will ever see the kind of tourist pressure out of Egmont that they have in New Zealand. As for mountains, Princess Louisa has them all beat, and during a heavy rain you can count over sixty waterfalls if the clouds don't hide them. It isn't too easy to find mountains that go all the way up to six thousand feet from their base in the ocean to the top, and the narrowness of the inlet and the height of the mountains on each side makes it seem like their feet almost touch. On the south side there is no vegetation to speak of, and it looks like slate from water's edge to their lofty tops. One of the inlet's beauties to me is the stillness. You can see every detail mirrored in the waters. To the left of Chatterbox Falls, if you let your eyes go upward, there is an overhanging bluff, and if the moisture content of the air is just right, standing under the overhang is a cowboy alongside his horse. (Most of the time it doesn't show.) On a sunny day with those beautiful mountains covered with snow, I think Princess Louisa will hold its own with Milford Sound or anyplace else in the world.

After Charles Roscoe Johnstone and his family left Princess Louisa around the end of World War I, the only person living in the inlet was Herman Casper. His full name was Herman Alwin Harry Casper and he was born in Germany on February 4, 1887. His story of how he had to desert the German army and seek refuge in Switzerland has been questioned as being made up to get sympathy. However, it could possibly be true. He would have had to go into the army at age eighteen for two years compulsory service, and at the end of the two years he decided to make a career of it and claimed he advanced to the rank of sergeant-major. He said he knocked a superior officer out cold in an altercation, and as that could have resulted in the death penalty, he deserted and escaped to Switzerland then to Canada. After a short time he found Princess Louisa Inlet and decided to make his permanent home in this lovely place. He built a cabin right by the narrows and made a living mostly handlogging, sometimes in the early days as the partner of Charlie Whittaker, who lived

Herman Casper was living like a hermit in the area that eventually became the Malibu Club. For a while after World War I, Herman was the only person living in the inlet. COURTESY LINDA MATTIS

across the inlet from Princess Louisa, and sometimes with Charlie Trebett.

A lot of people dropped in on Herman Casper and always found him friendly, and he had a lot of cats to keep him company. He was a well-educated man who could turn his hand to anything of a mechanical nature. He played a zither, which was handmade, as well as a handmade guitar, and he composed some of his own tunes. One was called, "The Princess Louisa Waltz" and another "The Soaring Eagle Polka." Linda Mattis, Charlie Whittaker's granddaughter, has one of his recordings. He was a close personal friend of the Whittakers and James "Mac" MacDonald, who helped him get his music recorded, and when Joyce Whittaker had to spend time in a Vancouver hospital, he wrote letters of encouragement to her.

Herman Casper died on June 14, 1969, after a two-week stay at St. Mary's hospital. He was buried in the Seaview Cemetery in Gibsons.

Nobody else lived in Princess Louisa until around 1927 when James Fredrick MacDonald bought the land around the famous tourist attraction, Chatterbox Falls, for $420. He was the American businessman that M. Wylie "Capi" Blanchet described in her book *The Curve of Time* (Blackwood & Sons, 1961) as "the man from California." The locals and all his many friends called him "Mac." He hired the McNaughton brothers—Bill and Don—and their father, Jack, and his brother Dan, who were loggers and excellent builders and axemen and had access to cedar logs, to build him a special log house. After I met Bill, the oldest brother, in 1955, he told me that Mac spared no expense in the construction of that log house. It had a huge living room, twenty by forty feet, with a high ceiling held up with two-foot-diameter cedar logs for beams, and an axe-hewn log stairway leading up to the bedrooms. Even the furniture was made with an axe. Bill and

Mac in his first years in Princess Louisa Inlet. COURTESY PRINCESS LOUISA SOCIETY

Mac's cabin was built entirely of cedar logs. This photo shows the twenty-by-forty-foot living room and the davenport in front of the fireplace. The bedrooms were upstairs. COURTESY PRINCESS LOUISA SOCIETY

his brother Don loved building the house, and they gave Mac a home he could be proud of. He spent as much time here as he could, and when he wasn't entertaining his many friends who came to call, he really enjoyed the solitude and peace of the place. One winter he left Steve Johnstone in his house as watchman while he went south. When he got back, he found Steve had used all the firewood and stripped a lot of the siding off the back of the house to keep the fire going.

The Great Crab Race

I have heard from several sources that in the 1940s and 1950s, when there were at least a dozen logging camps working in the inlet, a big picnic was organized some years, sometimes for May 24. A place was picked and word sent out so everyone could be prepared. Liquid lubrication had to be ordered well ahead. Sometimes a big crowd of people—wives, kids and all—came all the way from the head, and a few came from as far down as Egmont to attend. These were hard-working loggers and their wives, living miles apart in the north half of Jervis, so these were good breaks from the lives they lived and gave people a chance to visit. Everyone brought food and refreshments. A big camp was chosen for the picnic so as to have enough room for games and tents if necessary, as the picnic usually lasted into the next day. They would run races and play games and have a great time socializing together. Some of these friendships lasted long after the old-timers retired and left Jervis Inlet.

Sometimes the great highlight of picnic day was the crab race. Each camp had their contestant, a beach crab, hand-picked and trained to the peak of physical perfection (with spares in case of leg sprain) and carrying the camp colours across their backs. A big circle was drawn in the dirt, and all the crabs were put under a tub turned upside down in the centre. The tub was lifted straight up so that no crab had the advantage, and they were off with a lot of side betting and yelling to encourage their camp's crab to strain to the utmost. The first one to reach the line won the trophy.

The first crab race was the brainchild of old Mac MacDonald and was run along the lines of the Kentucky Derby at Mac's place at the head of Princess Louisa. Mac said he picked the idea out of the blue when it was his turn to organize the annual picnic. He got some young men to help him build a twelve-foot diameter sand track. The judge sat on a raised seat with three seats for the board of governors alongside. Someone made a betting window to add to the racetrack atmosphere. After everyone was full of delicious food, they all assembled around the ring. Right on cue Herman Casper fired an old sawed-off gun, and the starter up on his seat dropped the rock that made the tub fly up in the air, releasing the crabs. So the race was on, to the noisy encouragement of the various owners. Len Eilel's "Buster Crabbe" made it to the finish line first in record time, followed by Whittaker's "Patrick." But Mac got two young loggers to protest on the grounds of the gender of the winner as the rules called for stallion crabs only. The judge, who was flabbergasted, turned the decision over to the board of governors, who rendered a decision worthy of Solomon. They noted that the lack of hair on Buster's shell showed a feminine tendency, but the strong growth of hair on its chest showed the male strain was definitely present. Summing the matter up, the board ruled that "Buster Crabbe" was 60 percent male and the winner. (The McNaughtons' crab, "Three Star Hennesey" with jockey "Willie Survive," didn't place.) The crowd went wild, or so Mac reported of the first Princess Louisa sweepstake race.

Mac's house burned down about 1940. The fire may have been the result of him leaving a dishtowel hanging where it could have fallen on the stove, which he had left going to keep the house warm for his wife. She was waiting for him at Brittain River, just off the Union boat. When they got around the first bend in Princess Louisa, they could see the smoke. She was a city girl from California and the stress of living in a tent after that caused her to get an extreme case of shingles, and she spent time in a Vancouver hospital. She found her way back to civilization, and any hope of her ever going to Princess Louisa again was gone, so Mac bought a floating scow house that he anchored to the shore and spent all his summers there alone. He used to have it towed to Pender Harbour for the winter, and someone kept an eye on it, though sometimes he rented it to a reliable person for the winter.

Malibu

Thomas Hamilton, an American who patented the variable pitch airplane propeller and made millions as a partner in Hamilton Beech Aircraft Ltd., also fell in love with Princess Louisa and in the mid-1930s purchased all the available property around the inlet, including the island that bore his name. He even paid Herman Casper for his squatter's rights then let him live there as long as he wanted. No record can be found that Casper ever owned the property, but Hamilton paid him four hundred dollars for his house, which he said was full of fleas from all Casper's cats, and Casper moved across to the other side of the narrows where he lived for the rest of his life. Hamilton spared no expense to build his dream, the Malibu Club, on the property at the mouth of Princess Louisa Inlet. He made it into a beautiful chalet-style lodge, where he could have a world-class clientele. He even found enough room on the little peninsula for a golf course. When his resort was fully operational in 1941, he had two or three big Fairmile-sized boats and several smaller vessels to move guests and supplies. A lot of famous people were seen there—even movie actors like Bing Crosby and John Wayne.

But with World War II starting, his resort's opening

was badly timed and after a few years of operating in the red, Hamilton shut it down. Roy Dusenbury from Pender Harbour had been boat man as well as maintenance man for the lodge, and he and his wife, Doris, stayed on for a while as watchmen. In 1954 Hamilton sold the lodge to the Young Life Society, a Christian group that specializes in teen camps, for $350,000 and I've heard he even forgave some of that.

Mac MacDonald was always welcome at the Young Life camp, as he really enjoyed being around young people and always had some kind of a funny story or humorous antic to pull. It was said that once he gave up a breakfast invitation on Arthur Godfrey's big yacht to keep his weekly appointment to paddle down the inlet in his red canoe, dressed as an Indian, to perform his Native dance for the young folks. They say his last Indian fire dance ended with the curtains in the room catching fire, so he couldn't do that one anymore.

The Princess Louisa International Society

Princess Louisa was almost sacred to Mac, and as he got older and worried that his beloved spot would fall into private hands to become who-knows-what, he gave it to a yachtsmen's association, the Princess Louisa International Society, and they made it into a marine park. Mac's final summer in Princess Louisa was 1972, when he was the honoured guest of Young Life at Malibu. He spent his final years in a Seattle nursing home, where he died in 1978 at eighty-nine years of age. The Society gave the park to the BC government in 1963 and it's now part of the provincial parks system. They purchased Hamilton Island and renamed it MacDonald Island in memory of old Mac. (Bruce Calhoun's book called *Mac and the Princess* (Ricwalt Publishing, 1947) is out of print.)

Since they took over Malibu, the Young Life Society handles close to four hundred kids a week. They added a huge gymnasium and a lot of new buildings and went completely green by harnessing a river across Jervis Inlet that will meet the lodge's power needs for the foreseeable future. One guy told me it had already paid for itself in diesel fuel savings.

From Young Life's dock in Egmont, the *Malibu Princess* takes the kids up there in one load and also runs day trips for the general public. The ever-increasing yachting traffic has made the beautiful Princess Louisa Inlet a number-one world destination, so every summer more people take the Malibu guided tours. The souvenir store does a good business, and the profits help to defray expenses. Young Life also have a camp in the inlet behind MacDonald Island up toward the head where they run an Outward Bound-type of advanced program, involving hikes overnight up to the six-thousand-foot level of the surrounding mountains.

The McNaughton Brothers

The first time I saw Bill and Don McNaughton was when they came to Fred Klein's place at the head of Pender Harbour to visit their cousin Jean, who had married my Uncle Fred. Jean's father, Dan McNaughton, was brother to Jack or John McNaughton, the father of Bill and Don. Dan and Jack McNaughton had been loggers in New Brunswick, and after the logging there started to peter out, they had come west with another Scottish family, the Goods, to chase gold in the Yukon for a few years before they moved to BC. Most of the Goods stayed in the Yukon, but Nettie Good left her abusive husband and wound up at Garden Bay where she met my uncle, Fred Klein. They had four children, but she died of complications in her last pregnancy. So Fred's second wife, Bill and Don's cousin Jean, had known the folks of his first wife, the Goods, in the Yukon.

The McNaughtons had a logging outfit near the north end of Jervis Inlet as well as other places in Jervis, but in their early days here the brothers Dan and Jack and Jack's sons, Bill and Don, all worked together. At one time they had two camp tenders, the *Nighthawk* and the *Blackhawk*, so I guess they had a fair-sized gypo operation. Then old Jack and his wife

Left to right: Bill, Marge and Don McNaughton. Bill and Don built Mac's log cabin using only axes. COURTESY GRACE EVICH

retired to Secret Cove. Dan moved across the inlet and mostly handlogged on his own for many years. His daughter Jean became a teacher but was unable to get a job, so she moved up Jervis with her dad for a few years until she got the school in Kleindale. That's where she met and married Fred Klein. Fred and Jean had three kids, Bill, Grace and Jimmy. When Dan got too old to log, he moved in with his daughter and his grandchildren.

With the exception of the time spent in the Canadian army's forestry corps in World War II, Bill and Don McNaughton were woodsmen and trappers all their lives and did some extraordinary things when they were younger. My dad told me that one day when he was booming for a camp in Theodosia Inlet in Desolation Sound these two guys with packs on their backs came walking down the road. It was Bill and Don McNaughton. They had hiked across the mountains from the head of Jervis Inlet just for the fun of it. But one of their trapping adventures almost cost them their lives.

They had always heard about the trail to Squamish through the Elaho River valley that the Natives used, and they thought there would be lots of fur-bearing animals to catch in there, so after going in and building a cabin, Bill stayed there while Don went out and hired a plane to fly in enough supplies for the winter. Everything went as planned, and when the plane found the cabin, Bill had marked the drop area well. After the stuff was all dropped in the snow, Don flew out and began hiking back in to spend the winter trapping. The only trouble was that they didn't reckon on the snow being so deep, and when the supplies hit, they dove right under the snow and most of the things they needed to survive were gone. On top of this, even with snowshoes it took Don nearly a month to make it back and find the place, and Bill was in such bad shape by then he could hardly speak. They found it was hard to walk in that deep powder snow so they were unable to trap many animals. As the months passed and the food began to run out, they were facing starvation. They ate the animals they caught, but that was a losing proposition. What saved them was the fact that the BC Game Department had transplanted some elk to McNab Creek, away up Howe Sound, and they had spread into the Elaho Valley. The boys were able to shoot a big one and survive until the snow melted enough for them to walk out. Bill said it took a long time to get over the ordeal.

About 1953 Bill and Don McNaughton, who did some handlogging and had a Cat show at one time, sold out I think to Rod Webb and retired to Pender Harbour. They bought a place out on the end of Francis Peninsula Road where they had a view of the whole Malaspina Strait and the mouth of Agamemnon Channel. They could look up the channel and see the lovely snow-covered mountains of

Jervis Inlet, and they had time to experiment with guns and shooting. They had a gun vice and range and were handloading their own cartridges to get better accuracy. They were able to shoot three shot groups as small as three-eighths of an inch at a hundred yards with a 222-calibre rifle and a 6 +24 power scope. I got acquainted with them through the Pender Harbour Gun Club, which they were anxious to see formed, and about eight of us held the first memberships. We got some steel backstops made and started the Dominion Marksman program in the community hall. Don's cousin Grace Evich has his Dominion Marksman shield with a nearly perfect score, 5,078 out of 6,000 bull's eyes at forty-five feet; two thousand were offhand.

The McNaughton boys were very community-minded, and Bill served on the water board with me for a number of years, and we worked well together and became good friends. But retirement didn't set too well with the brothers so they started hunting seals, mostly on the upper BC coast in the *Nighthawk* with a gas engine. They would turn in between five hundred and a thousand noses a year for the five dollar bounty—this was back when seals were considered a nuisance. The McNaughtons just loved being on the water, and after a few years they re-powered their boat with a small diesel engine and went to work for the Department of Fisheries, patrolling the west coast of the Queen Charlotte Islands in the fishing season. When their Fisheries contract ran out, they went back to hunting seals for the bounty.

From time to time the brothers would show 16-mm movies they had made of their hikes in the backcountry of Jervis and other places. I have often wondered what happened to the many hours of black-and-white film they

Bill shot this record-sized grizzly bear up the Skwakwa River while running his trapline. The bear was extremely old, had bad teeth and was in such poor condition that his hair was falling out and going grey around the head.

COURTESY GRACE EVICH

had. Eventually when they were along in years, they both got married. Don married Nan, the oldest McKay girl, and they bought the old Farquarson place, about three hundred feet from where Nan had been raised in "Hardscratch," the Scottish settlement in Whiskey Slough, Pender Harbour. Bill married a lady called Edith from Chemainus, and they lived in the boys' old place at the end of Francis Peninsula Road. They were still sometimes called on by the Fishery Department to shoot seals when they were causing trouble up the coast. In his last years Don suffered from Alzheimers; Bill lived into his late eighties. The two brothers had remained the best of friends, and from the time of their move to the Coast, they had spent most of their long lives in Jervis Inlet. They were true pioneers.

Other Residents of Queens Reach, Jervis Inlet

Among the other people who spent most of their working lives in Jervis and considered it home was a Norwegian logger named Nels Erickson, who was partners in a logging camp with Pete Hanson for many years. Pete's wife, Lottie, had four children by her first husband, Charlie Wise, who was drowned in a boating accident, along with their oldest son. Then Pete and Lottie had another five children—although Nels, the second Hanson boy, looked so much different than the rest of their kids that people suspected the two partners shared more than a logging company. Nels Hanson and his brother Pete worked for me and my partner, Bob O. Lee, on Texada Island in 1960. Nels was about six foot three and wiry and tough, and with his long legs he went through the woods like a moose. He was always waiting for me to catch up when we went cruising timber together.

One day in 1965, Jack Gooldrup phoned to see if I would take him up to the end of Jervis for a fishing trip. I needed a break so we cranked up the old *Dakota Belle*, the school ferry I was running at the time. The old girl was long and narrow and cruised at ten knots so we made the forty-mile trip in four hours. Jack knew Nels Erickson, Pete Hanson's old partner, who still lived at the head of the inlet. People who have lived in the isolation of Queens Reach, surrounded by the beautiful mountains of Jervis Inlet, are often loath to leave. As well, lifelong friendships developed so there was sort of a sense of community, and even though they lived some distance from each other, they looked out for their neighbours. Nels Erickson loved that place so much that he lived there for years after he retired, until old age and health issues forced him to go back to civilization.

So we dropped in on old Nels and were invited to spend the night there. We stayed up well into the night yarning about past experiences, then got up early and went fishing with rod and reel. Jack was one of those dedicated sportsmen who had a tackle box full of proven lures. I had borrowed stuff from my brother-in-law, which he thought was the finest. (A lot of the lures we buy are very pretty, and they work well to catch the suckers that buy them.) Jack out-fished me four to one that day, and we caught our limit trolling along the drop-off at the end of the inlet. But we kept getting a huge strike that always broke off. One of the plugs we lost came floating up with no hook left, and Jack said that Basil Joe told him it was the "Hunaechin Monster." It always struck in the same spot near a windfall on the beach. Jack said that on one of the trips he took with Basil, when they were fishing the same tack and Basil was steering the boat, he always gave the Hunaechin Monster a wide berth. Most likely it was the big ling cod that Basil claimed swallowed the little girl who was swimming with some other Native kids years before. Some ling cod reach a hundred pounds, and rockfish have been found to reach eighty-five years old. So the monster got a few of our lures that day.

Basil Joe told me that smallpox epidemics took a terrible toll on the Native peoples of Jervis Inlet, and he said the people were dying so fast that they were unable to bury them all. They put the bodies in the large cave on the right side at the head of Jervis Inlet under the foot of Hunaechin Mountain, so the top end of Jervis is a special place for Native memories.

For a few years in the 1970s, the Sechelt Nation had a school at Tsonei where teenagers from the Peninsula could come and learn about some of the Native culture along with their regular school work. Some of the kids who benefitted from the program were white. Our youngest daughter is an adopted Tsimshian girl from the Skeena River area. When she got into her early teens, she began to have problems with self-worth and identity, so we enrolled her in this school, and I think it did help her. It is hard enough being adopted without facing some of the bigotry that is still out there for a Native kid to face. She is doing very well now, married with a son. She says she's a Mackintosh—Indian red on the outside and white on the inside—so we are grateful for that school. The program has been cancelled, as it is too expensive for transportation.

Minnie Solberg and her man, Harry Dray, lived down by Deserted Bay where Queens Reach meets Princess Royal Reach. They loved it so much that they still wanted to stay when medical problems would have sent anyone else out to civilization. Harry finally died, but still Minnie wouldn't leave. Her sister was the "Cougar Lady," Bergliot "Bergie" Solberg, who made her home a few miles up Sechelt Inlet from Porpoise Bay. The two girls were taught by their father from the earliest age to be self-supporting wilderness women. Their father had built a gillnet boat years before with the idea of going to Rivers Inlet in the summer, but I don't think he ever made it there. The boat sat at Porpoise Bay for years after he passed away; I don't know if the girls could even run it. Bergie owned small runabouts, but I don't think they were suitable to make it up to Deserted Bay, so after Harry died, Minnie had no way to get supplies, and Bergie would prevail on someone to take her up there to visit with an order of food and sometimes medicine. A lot of other people were keeping their eyes on her, too, or she wouldn't have been able to stay as long as she did. Ronnie and Diane Fenn were her nearest neighbours, and John Daly, with his wife Edith, would go up there and spend Christmas with her. I think she had a radio phone and was in contact with someone who could reach the phone tower to call for her.

A Close Call

In 1962 my partner Bob Lee and I looked at the timber in the untouched valley of Lansman Creek, the last valley on the west side of Jervis, two and a half miles from the end of Queens Reach. We spent a day up there looking at the timber, but due to the size of the claim, we'd been unable to make it to the far end. Rod Webb, an experienced retired logger, was thinking of helping to finance the deal, so to kill two birds with one stone, Bob and Rod chartered a Supercub on floats that was flying out of Pender Harbour. The pilot was a guy who we later found out was nicknamed "Crazy Olson." They were flying along at 2,500 feet, and when Bob said they were at Lansman, Olson hung a left up the valley. The back of this valley was 1,800 feet in elevation with a steep, high mountain on each side. It was a hot day, and there was a creek in the bottom of the valley and shade on the south side, so the air was just pouring down the valley, and as soon as they began to get in there, the altimeter started to drop. Even with full climb, they were sinking, and as they got further in, it was too narrow to make the turn to get out, and it looked like they were doomed. Olson may have been a bit crazy, but he could sure fly a plane. He managed to do one of those Immelmann turns, where you pull the plane up and let it fall over sharply to the left. Bob said when the turn was completed, the plane was right down to the treetops.

Not too long after this, Olson lost his pilot's licence. It seems he had a history of epileptic fits, but he could feel them coming on and wouldn't fly that day. He had managed to hide it from the DOT inspectors to get his commercial pilot's licence.

The Whittaker Family

Another of the old characters who lived in Jervis was Charlie Whittaker. He was born on May 13, 1884, at Belmount, Hawkshead, in Lancaster, England, and the family emigrated to Washington State when he was three years old and then moved to BC in 1906. When I knew him, Charlie was a tall, rawboned, no-nonsense kind of a guy who didn't tolerate much BS. He had most likely been a regular logger type in his first years in BC, and the order

Bruce (holding oars) and Neil Whittaker in a rowboat. COURTESY LINDA MATTIS

of the day then was that you made your stake, and when winter camp closure came, you went to the city till the camps opened again. A dozen of the hotels on Water Street would advertise as "Your home away from home," so most of the loggers could be found in that area that's known today as "Gastown." It was named after John (Gassy Jack) Deighton, who was the first saloon owner in what became Vancouver in 1886. Charlie liked to stay at Tommy Roberts' Grand Hotel as Roberts was known to be trustworthy, and the loggers could put their money in his safe, and he would dole it out to them as they needed it. A logger packing his summer's stake on his person would usually get rolled by thieves, and he would find his holiday cut short and end up on the old *Cassiar*, the loggers' boat, heading back to a camp with a big headache. Loggers were often heard to say that they had spent their money on wine, women and song—and the rest foolishly. Roberts also ran a hiring hall for loggers, where camps could post their positions to fill on a big blackboard, and there were other hiring halls in walking distance of the Union Steamship wharf.

Ethel and Charlie Whittaker married in November 1913, and Ethel followed Charlie into the wilds of Jervis Inlet. COURTESY LINDA MATTIS

Charlie met Ethel May Hawkey in 1913; she had come over from England alone and after some time found the

"PININ"
Smoke a'driftin; shadows shiftin;
Sleigh bells tinklin' down the lane'
Sun a' sinkin; me a' thinkin'
Bout you comin' back again.
Snow a' fallin; birds a' callin;
Winds a'moanin' in the pine;
Day is dying; hon I'm sighin'
For a little hand in mine.

Dusk a' stealin; got a' feelin'
that you're kinda lonesome too;
Ain't you missing' me a'kissin'
You, just like I used to do?
Day so dreary, been so weary,
Ever since you went away;
Just a' griven', 'bout you leavin'
Wantin' you this weary day;

C.E.W.

Charlie Whittaker wrote a poem for his wife Ethel during the long periods when they were apart. She was living in Vancouver with the kids, and he was working in Jervis. PHOTO AND POEM: LINDA MATTIS only job available was in the Grand Hotel as a chambermaid. They married in November 1913. He was a good cook and taught Ethel, who was a good pupil. It must have taken a lot of courage to follow Charlie up to the wilds of Jervis Inlet where by that time he had a handlogging claim in Queens Reach. In those first years the only other women would have been Dora Johnstone across the inlet in Princess Louisa and a few Native ladies at Deserted Bay, though eventually the McNaughtons moved nearby with a logging camp. On September 5, 1914, Charlie and Ethel's first child, Henry Hawkey, was born; a daughter, Joyce Minnie, was born on January 6, 1916. Charlie built a nice house on the beach above Patrick Point, which became their home until their two kids needed to go to school, and the Whittakers bought a house in Vancouver. After that, Charlie had to stay up Jervis alone for long periods. One of these times he wrote a poem for Ethel.

In December 1933 Joyce—who could log side by side

Charlie and his kids, Henry and Joyce, at Queens Reach, Jervis Inlet. The three of them logged side by side. COURTESY LINDA MATTIS

Henry Whittaker's first boat was the Gypsy No. 3. COURTESY LINDA MATTIS

The Prelude *was Henry Whittaker's second boat.* COURTESY LINDA MATTIS

with her dad and Henry—had an accident, most likely in the woods, that was serious enough to send her to St. Paul's Hospital. Ethel thought she was turning into a tomboy, and to provide an incentive toward more female pursuits, she and Joyce moved down to Pender Harbour where they rented the "White House" in Lee's Bay at Irvines Landing. Henry and Charlie would come down from the camp, and we often would

Henry and Jean Whittaker eventually got into the tourist business in Pender Harbour. COURTESY LINDA MATTIS

see them when we went for the mail on boat days. Ethel was very British-sounding, and I remember her putting on airs with her nose a bit in the air and acting like she was a cut above the common lot of us. Old Charlie would put her in her place by reminding her that when they met she was just a chambermaid in the Grand Hotel where the standard conveniences were one bathroom per floor, a pitcher of water, a porcelain basin and a thunder mug. Henry and his dad became partners in Whittaker Logging Co. and went on for a few more years handlogging together. Joyce married Norman Lee, and before Charlie retired, he had the Gooldrup brothers build a nice house for him on the hillside above Joyce's place overlooking Lee's Bay. They called it Belmount after his birthplace in England. His son Henry took over his logging interests after he retired, but they got into a dispute over money that left them estranged for many years; fortunately they patched it up before Charlie had a stroke and Ethel couldn't physically handle him anymore. By this time Henry and Jean were in the tourist business in Pender Harbour, so Henry was on hand to look after his dad until he died in 1961 at seventy-seven years of age.

I was told a funny story about Henry, who was not known

for being overly generous with money. Norman Lee's brother, Bob H. Lee, who told me this story, had gone to school with Henry. After World War II Bob was always short of cash, having returned from overseas and getting married and just starting a family. Most of the veterans were starting from nothing, while those (like Henry) who didn't have to go in the army were much better off. Henry was now logging with a gas donkey and a Cat and needed a few men to help him. Bob had the notion that, if he went to a camp, he would get free rent and save some money, so he moved his family up to the Whittakers' camp and worked there for six months. He found the cost of living and unplanned expenses forced him to get the odd drag on future wages, so when he went to get his final paycheque, the "de ducks"—as he called them—took everything but $1.38. So he took the cheque, framed it and hung it on the wall. He had to admit that Henry had paid him to the penny everything he had promised, but he got a lesson on accounting when Henry contacted him to ask him to cash the cheque as it was preventing him from making his books balance. But many of the friends and neighbours from Jervis would drop in on Jean and Henry over the years that they ran the resort at Farrington Cove and found them great hosts. Bea and Harold Swanson, past friends from Deserted Bay, were sometimes their guests.

A Change in the Weather

My friend Rod Webb, who lived year-round at the head of Jervis Inlet, always felt that Patrick Point, the last point on the west side at the beginning of Queens Reach, was the meeting place between interior and coastal weather systems. He had radio contact with someone outside, and many days it would be rainy and miserable farther west but not a cloud in the sky to the north. He would be bragging about wearing shirt sleeves basking in the sun on Christmas day. But at the head of Jervis, you are halfway through the Coast Range and into interior weather patterns, so it made sense to me.

Mining in the Jervis Inlet Area

Not far inland from the end of Hotham Sound is one of the most spectacular mountains in the lower Jervis area, six-thousand-foot Mount Diadem, which can be seen clearly from the mouth of Agamemnon Channel. When covered with snow, it looks like an ice cream cone with the southwest side nearly vertical. Over the years there's been a lot of mining activity in the Mount Diadem area and at the head of Hotham Sound, and in the Depression years some of the men from Egmont packed in supplies for a prospector for a dollar a day.

Dad seemed to have a great interest in mining, often mentioning the names of the prospectors in the inlet. He claimed that an old guy named Sandy Marrs or de Marrs had a gold mine somewhere on this mountain, but it must have been quite far up because he had to wait until the snow melted off to start every year. He packed his supplies in from the end of the Sound and didn't come out until fall with his gold. He didn't get much but kept going back year after year hoping for a big strike, so he must have got enough to live on. There were copper claims in the same Mount Diadem area, and my dad always talked about Baramba Mines that had a big wharf at the head of Hotham Sound when he first moved to Jervis Inlet in 1920. Though they spent a lot of money on tunnelling, it seemed to fizzle out. A guy named Harry Jolley also had a mine in this area.

Dad also talked about Paddy Hatt, Ben Coates, Teddy Groven and Tom Lillie. Paddy Hatt had a trapline in the mountains north of Princess Louisa, but he also prospected up Treat or Beaver Creek. Ben Coates drove a forty-foot tunnel into the mountainside above Jack Bay but never seems to have shipped any ore. He lived for a time on what we locals called Blakely's Island, and my dad said Ben once told him he came to BC from the US where he was wanted for murder. He had been a US marshal for many years and had spent a lot of time trying to catch a famous outlaw, but after he left the lawman's job, he ran into this outlaw and killed him. This would have been fine for a lawman, but he was no longer wearing the badge, so he was a wanted man and headed across the border and never looked back. It is recorded that he died in 1942 at the age of 101 years, still expecting to find the rich vein. Now that's a real prospector.

Paddy Hatt, a prospector and miner, spent a lot of his time in Jervis Inlet.
COURTESY BRENDA SILVEY

Tom Lillie lived beside Lillie's Lake in Pender Harbour. He and Teddy Groven staked claims way up on Mount Diadem in 1918 but were forced out by forest

Egmont community picnic, Emerson Creek, 1934. Back row, left to right: Bob Jefferies, Alfred Jefferies, Don Gilmore, Ben Coates, Abe Jefferies. Front row, left to right: Bill Anderson, Bill Griffith, George Vaughan. COURTESY EGMONT HERITAGE CENTRE

fires the next year and then the bottom fell out of the minerals market. Lillie died of a heart attack walking home from Donley's store in 1923. Lately some great mysterious name-changer decided that the local name of Lillie's Lake was not fitting, so they changed it to Paq Lake. But it was named for Tom Lillie, not the flowers that are growing so profusely in its shallow waters. Somehow Jim Warnock, one of the old-timers, took exception to this change and made enough of a fuss that he got it changed back to Lillie's Lake. Jim felt Tom Lillie should be remembered. Teddy Groven went on prospecting around Brittain River but never found anything. When he went missing in 1938, his wife was able to flag down the Columbia Coast Mission boat *Rendezvous*, and they found his body in his rowboat a ways down the inlet. Over the years I have heard Jimmy Archibald mentioned as another guy who did a lot of prospecting in Jervis Inlet when he wasn't handlogging.

Ernie Pendergast was another old prospector that my dad mentioned. He had a claim away up above Killam Bay, just inside Lone Tree or Miller Island. Then there is Ernie Silvey's mine, just north of Agamemnon Bay. It was very close to the beach and partly on a reef that is almost touching the beach. And there was a great deal of excitement forty years ago when one of the Vancouver Stock Exchange promoters stirred up some good reports to raise capital. It was supposed to be an extension of the gold vein that Silvey had found.

I can remember my dad taking a few of us kids to the sand beach just east of what we call Cockrill Bay between Captain Island and Vanguard Bay on Nelson Island to look for an abandoned prospect about five hundred feet up from the beach. He wasn't too long finding this big hole in the ground, about fifteen feet across and ten feet deep. It looked like it had been a lot deeper at one time but had sloughed in. We found some small chunks of a silvery metal that looked like lead though harder and shinier, but there wasn't enough for an assay. But after he died, I found out he had hired one of my cousins in Egmont to take him to the same spot again. One day I was talking to Red Nicholson, the owner of the water taxi *White Arrow*, and he said a guy hired him to take him to the same spot and wait for most of the day while he searched for something, so there must be some good reports about this area.

When we were logging in Vanguard Bay, I had to go from Earls Cove to our claim in Vanguard alone one Sunday to do some work on the Cat so it would be ready to work on Monday. I was finished about two in the afternoon, but by then it was very foggy. We had all our courses and times written down, but they were all taken with two or more people in a fifteen-foot outboard at full throttle, so with only one man on board I made a lot more distance on the long leg between Vanguard and Captain Island and missed the gap between Nelson and Captain islands. So when my time was up, I ran south until I could see a beach through the thick fog. As I followed what I assumed was the beach on Captain Island, I could see a big hole in the bluff a few feet above the beach that looked to me to be the portal of a tunnel. After that I followed the beach to what I thought must be the east end of Captain Island, took a south course into Agamemnon Bay and slowly followed the beach down to the Earls' float and then home. I have looked for this tunnel since to no avail. The point being that, if there is one missing adit, there are many more in the length of this highly mineralized inlet, and it may be time to revisit some of these old claims. With the price of metals today, who knows whether there may be something worth a second look?

There was also some good placer ground found at the upper end of the inlet. During World War I the Canadian government sent miners to check out some platinum that was found by placer mining in one of the creeks not far below Princess Louisa Inlet. My son Wilf found out about this while doing research at Simon Fraser. He was so interested that he and friends made a trip up there and hiked up the creek. The going was so rough it took them all day. They looked around and left, always intending to come back but never did.

My uncles Pete and John Klein found some very rich copper ore on the top of the mountain at Treat Creek, which was named after Henry Whitney Treat, an American who acquired claims up there then put in a wharf and an aerial tram from his mine to the beach. The ore was iron and copper, but the spark was gone when Treat died in 1920 before the mine was opened. It might be worth looking for now that there are logging roads nearly to the top of the mountain.

Up on Mount Halliwell is where my uncles Pete and John

leased their brother Fred Klein's property, and after building a road up to the 2,700-foot level, were successful in shipping out a little over seven hundred tons of high-grade copper ore to the smelter in Tacoma, Washington. They averaged over seventy dollars per ton and made money. But the ore body was very small, and when all the easy high-grade ore was gone, they shut it down. One of the big samples that they sent down to the Chamber of Mines was the second-best sample found in BC at that time. You could send electricity through that ore and pick native copper wire out of some samples. A Vancouver stock exchange company called Salurian Chieftain Mining Co. promoted stock on the Klein brothers' production, but they only produced another 150 tons and went bankrupt.

I guess the most successful mining operations in Jervis Inlet have been the gravel mines at Beaver Creek with Delta Rock and the one at the Skookumchuck. Think of all the gravel that has to be moved while placer mining for a bit of gold, and here they get paid for every yard of it that's moved! Orville Lawson operated a gravel mine further up the inlet but gave it up after a few years. Then there was the one on Cockburn beach that is no longer producing, but the loading works are still sticking up out there in the chuck, rusting away. It could become dangerous if it is not dismantled before it collapses. There is an abandoned lime quarry or mine not far from Judd Johnstone's house in Blind Bay, which operated for a while when Dad first lived in Jervis Inlet.

Log Barges

Logging activity on the coast is way down from the days of big clear-cuts and no-end-in-sight logging. Now it's getting closer to the one big company doing it in the most cost-effective way with very little competition to keep the stumpage returns to the government coffers up. The ups and downs in the market for our lumber has only speeded up this process. In the 1970s and into the 1980s there were three log barge dumping and sorting facilities in Jervis Inlet that employed a lot of men. Lew Milligan at Vanguard Bay, Fielding at Westmere, and I think Crown Zellerbach at Goliath Bay. The quiet waters of Jervis Inlet gave them a place where the big seas of the outer coast were behind them, and bundle booms of sorted logs could be safely towed the rest of the way from here to the storage grounds of Howe Sound and the lower Fraser River. But they all quit working around the same time, and I don't see as many log barges around anymore.

A lot of people think the forest industry on the Coast has no future, and as I look around in Jervis Inlet, I can see that most of the old growth has been taken, but all those big valleys that were logged out years ago are almost ready to start cutting again. While it won't be like it was in the good old days, I think the old inlet will go on giving us her wood for as long as we need it.

Towboats

From the first handloggers at the turn of the century right down to the present, it was the towboats that made it possible for the logging industry to function on this coast. Jervis Inlet could not have been developed without them, so while I am sure they had a monotonous and often thankless job, I tip my hat to the tugboat operators. Many times they spent long days here waiting for a storm to go down. Then they not only had to work all hours of the night to get the booms out, but they also had to bring all those boom chains back to make the next tow. They had to drive wooden plugs into the auger holes so that the toggles couldn't trip and cause a spill. They had to be sure that the name of the camp was painted on the head swifter so it could be identified wherever it was tied up later, and they had to count the logs every time they tied up to check for losses.

In the old days the handloggers would often ride the tug to town to make sure they got their money, but I have heard of loggers losing their whole boom when a dishonest broker took off with the result of many months' work. A good honest broker was vital and made it possible for loggers to get parts and supplies sent upcoast by guaranteeing that the bill would be paid. They also acted as an agent to get the best price possible for the logs, and they collected the money from the mill. So when a logger got a good broker, he kept him.

Water Transportation to the Camps

Part of the introduction to the book *The Good Company: An Affectionate History of the Union Steamships* by Tom Henry (Harbour, 1994) says:

> Between 1889 and 1959 the vessels of the Union Steamship Company bound the coast together—and the company's red and black funneled steamers and their trademark whistle, one long, two shorts and a long, were a fixture of weekly life at virtually every logging camp, cannery and stump ranch between Vancouver and the Alaska panhandle.

There were so few camps in Jervis in May 1892 when the Union Steamships' *Comox*, the first steel ship to be built on the BC coast, went into service, that the inlet was ignored, although the boat called in at Pender Harbour about twice a month on its way to camps all the way north to Port Neville. By the time my dad moved to the Sunshine Coast in 1919, you could row out to meet the boat in front of your place or at one of the logging camps they serviced. The *Chilco* and the

The Comox *was one of the first Union boats to bring regular mail, freight and passenger service to Jervis Inlet through Pender Harbour. This was likely taken around 1900, when Irvine owned the first store.* COURTESY GORDON KLEIN

Chasina, the two ships Union Steamships took over when they bought out the All Red Line in 1917, serviced lower Jervis Inlet after that date, according to the limited needs of the camps, but a map of the Union routes shows that their scheduled runs never went past Brittain River until much later. Harold Wray of Egmont had a contract to go to Pender for the mail at least weekly, so I guess Union service to Egmont was not that regular, and most of the camps had their own camp tenders and would go to Pender on a regular basis. Dad ran one called *Lapan* for some time. Over the years a lot of guys ran freight and passengers from the big freight shed at Irvines Landing where old Bill Matier was freight man. I remember a guy named Harvey Herd who hauled freight with a beautiful boat called *Aleeta*. Frank Fontaine hauled freight and passengers with the *Dangler* and did a bit of towing as

The Charkay *was owned by Charlie and Kay Harris, who also owned eight other towboats. They towed mostly log booms. The* Charkay *was used in Jervis, mostly for freight and passengers. Charlie and Kay owned and operated from the property east of Duncan Cove in Pender Harbour.* COURTESY GORDON AND LORNA KLEIN

well, and Charlie Harris, who owned a towboat company, which he operated from the property east of Duncan Cove in Pender Harbour, towed log booms and ran the *Charkay* up Jervis with freight and passengers.

In 1946 Davidson Marine started a fast service in competition with Union Steamships on the Jervis and Powell River run with the *Gulf Wing, Gulf Stream* and *Jervis Express*, and for the next five years Jervis Inlet had good service. They folded partly because one dark night in 1947 when there was a heavy sea and strong southeast wind the *Gulf Stream* hit Dinner Rock, just a mile south of Lund. The boat slipped off into deeper water after most of the passengers were taken aboard the fishpacker *Betty L*, but two women and three children were drowned. Crosses were erected on the top of the rock as a memorial.

Dana Ramsey's water taxi *White Arrow* started serving the

inlet in the 1950s. Later Red Nicholson took it over and operated it out of Pender Harbour. Then he sold the original boat and replaced it with a twenty-six-foot Turner, which was a lot faster and very seaworthy, and he could service Jervis Inlet as well as Nelson and Texada islands. By this time, the bigger camps all had big AM radio phones that could reach outside of the inlet, and they could order things for Red and his *White Arrow* to bring them. Often he worked in conjunction with Lloyd's Store in Garden Bay to make a grocery run, stopping where needed and sharing the cost. Sometimes he would run the health nurse making her rounds checking health needs. The St. Mary's Hospital doctors would use him to make calls and emergency runs, and he always gave good, competent and cheerful service. For many years Jimmie Stevens worked out of Earls Cove to service Jervis with the *Triangle Lady* and Berntsen's taxi at Egmont, so in the later years people had a lot more options.

The Gulf Wing, *owned by Davidson Marine, offered water transportation to the Jervis Inlet area. The* Jervis Express, *another of Davidson's boats, is in the background.* COURTESY GORDON AND LORNA KLEIN

Red Nicholson (middle), the owner of the water taxi White Arrow. *COURTESY THE SWAN FAMILY*

The White Arrow *started servicing Jervis Inlet in the 1950s.* *COURTESY THE SWAN FAMILY*

Some lives were lost when boats that were too small for the severe conditions often encountered in the inlet's long reaches were pressed past safe boating practices. Ernie Pohl went missing in Princess Royal Reach in the mid-1930s. In 1960 a friend of mine was one of the six loggers who set out from their logging camp just south of the Skookumchuck but never arrived in Sechelt. This had to be Jervis Inlet's worst marine disaster. The inlet nearly claimed two more when Les Kearley and his sister-in-law, Jean Trebett, headed out from Brittain River into a mean sea. The boat was one that Les had added some length to with plywood and fibreglass, but the design was faulty, and it started to come apart after just a short time of bucking the seas. Someone watching from the shore saw them disappear and went out in another boat and found them hanging on to the gas can, a lucky break. If I have learned nothing else about Jervis, it is that the weather can never be trusted.

The Jervis Express *competed with the Union Steamships on the Jervis and Powell River run.* COURTESY BEA SWANSON

Epilogue

As my dad got older, one of the things he loved to do was to find one of his favourite bays and just anchor there and enjoy it. These places he loved all his life were precious to him, and he has passed some of this on to me. Go up to the head of Jervis, and you may still find the loggers float there as we did a few years ago. Get up at the crack of dawn, and perhaps you will see a grizzly bear or a herd of elk feeding on the flats. If you walk up the road, be very careful as the bears are not far away. (Check to see if there are a lot of fresh droppings!) Look for the pictograph sites. Try to pick a sunny day so you can see all the way to the tops of these lofty mountains. Be sure to visit Freil Falls, and if you possibly can, anchor at Harmony Islands for the night. If you like to fish for trout, walk the half mile in to Lena Lake. Then there is always a feed of oysters if you have your fishing licence.

My favourite time to go up Jervis is in the winter when the mountains are covered with snow. I will never forget going up the inlet one clear winter day just as the sun was coming up. I was abreast of Lone Tree Island as the first rays of the morning sun struck the tops of the mountains and they turned a beautiful pink. The peaks lit up one after another, and rays of light played hide and seek behind them. Finally the whole scene was bathed in solid pink. It was perfect timing, and I am sure glad I didn't miss it. I have been all over the BC coast in my forty-odd years of fishing, and I surely haven't seen it all, but I can assure you that it doesn't get better than this. And it's right at our front door.

Acknowledgments

First, I have to thank my dad, Jim Phillips, for taking the time to pass on his stories of the time he lived and worked in Jervis Inlet. It was obvious that he had a special love for the place and a lot of good memories, which he passed on to his children. He started to write it all down in longhand, but lung cancer from a lifetime of smoking ended his life before he got it finished, and I promised him that I would try to pass it on. I have added my own memories and some interesting stories about the people who were a part of this time. Some of the other folks to be thanked for contributing their stories, writings, photos and encouragement are:

Linda Mattis, Charlie Whittaker's grandaughter, for photos and stories of Queens Reach.

Barbara (Silvey) Higgins for Portuguese Joe's history and tales of old Egmont.

Brenda Silvey for photos from the files of the Egmont and Pender Harbour Historical Society.

Gordon and Lorna Klein for photos.

Doug Milligan for photos and stories of Lew Milligan's operation and life in Jervis Inlet.

Acknowledgments

Dean Bosch for photos and the story of his dad, Johnnie's, life.

Bea Swanson for historic logging photos and her memories of the inlet as a girl in 1928.

My sister, Caroline Jepson (Newcombe), for the piece she wrote on the Newcombe family.

My cousin Kathy (Grace) Evich for photos of the McNaughton brothers.

Also the publishers, who are the real ones that make it a book, especially Mary White for all the photo scanning.

If I have missed anyone, my apologies and thanks.

—Ray Phillips

Index

Photographs indicated in **bold.**

Index

Index